EYE OF THE STORM

Noreen Riols

HODDER AND STOUGHTON
LONDON SYDNEY AUCKLAND TORONTO

British Library Cataloguing in Publication Data

Riols, Noreen
.Eye of the storm.—(Hodder Christian paperback)
1. Christian life
I. Title
248.4   BV4501.2

ISBN 0-340-34158-0

Hodder and Stoughton Editorial Office: 47 Bedford Square, London
WC1B 3DP

TO
JACQUES
and the children

You are my hiding place from every
storm of life . . .
You surround me with songs of
victory.
 (Psalm 32: 7) (The Living Bible)

CONTENTS

1	A Bolt from the Blue	9
2	Along With The Madding Crowd	16
3	Come and See	21
4	The Encounter	28
5	And Something Happened	37
6	From a Long Way Off	44
7	Revelation	49
8	Action Stations	53
9	The Counter Attack	60
10	An Empty Pill Box	65
11	The Phone Call	73
12	Journeying Together	80
13	I'm Coming	86
14	The Scoffer	93
15	'Pray if you Like'	102
16	Early One Morning	108
17	Never Lose Hope	117
18	A Song of Triumph	124
19	The Climax	135
20	Life Without End	147
21	Out of the Tunnel	157
	As a Parting Word	160

This is a true story.

All the events and situations actually happened.

However in order to respect privacy and shared confidence, some details and most of the names have been changed: the exceptions being the lay reader and the two pastors mentioned in Chapters 16 and 18 and all the members of my family.

1

A BOLT FROM THE BLUE

The shrill, high-pitched ringing of the telephone beside my bed brought me from the depths of a fitful sleep. Half opening my eyes, I saw the watery November sun seeping in through the gap in the curtains, but I didn't want to wake up. I didn't want to face another day. The drone of the telephone was insistent and I reluctantly stretched out my arm to pick up the receiver.

As I did so, I glanced down at the cot by my side. The baby was awake, his deep blue eyes gazing up at me, and my heart melted into a pool of love inside me.

"Kit," I murmured, "oh Kit!"

It was Sunday morning and he was just three days old.

Through a haze of sleep I heard the knife-grinder calling for customers as he drove slowly down the street. His voice mingled with those of women hurrying home from the market, their baskets bulging with the morning's shopping.

It was all so different from what I had known as a child and, as the clouds of sleep began to evaporate, I remembered nostalgically the Sunday morning stillness of an English suburban street.

"Hallo," I said drowsily into the receiver.

It was my father, calling from Essex.

"Are you all right?" he asked anxiously. "I can hardly hear you. This must be a very bad line."

There was nothing wrong with the line, I was the one who was all wrong. And I didn't want to talk.

"Sorry," I yawned, "I'm half-asleep."

"How's the baby?" he enquired, reassured.

I gazed once more into the cot, but his eyes had closed and the soft, regular breathing told me that he had fallen back to sleep.

"He's *beautiful*," I murmured.

"Here's your mother."

"How are you?" my mother's voice came down the line, anxious in her turn.

"Oh, just wonderful," I lied.

"What are you calling him?"

"Christopher Robert."

Robert had been her father's name and I knew that, for her, this new baby would be someone very special.

I put down the receiver and gazed out of the window. The trees were black and bare in the little square outside Paris round which the Hertford British Hospital buildings were clustered. The pale sun had stopped trying to break through and a grey dullness surrounded everything, including me. Tears began to creep slowly down my face and I didn't know why there was such a blankness, a heaviness inside me, like the weather outside. Instead of a new life beginning, I felt as if all life had stopped and I wanted to bury myself in the soil like the hyacinth bulbs I had planted only a few days before, and not surface until spring.

I couldn't understand it. Christopher was a beautiful, nine-pound baby. We all wanted him and already loved him and yet inside me there was this blackness, this hopelessness, this unwillingness to face the future.

There was a knock on the door and a slight, white-haired man came in.

"I'm the Catholic priest," he said shyly.

He smiled and his whole face lit up.

"I'm Protestant," I replied, a sudden ray of hope creeping into my heart; maybe this dear old man could help me, could tell me why I was feeling like this.

I smiled up at him but he backed away.

"Your own chaplain will be coming round," he said gently, "and there's an Anglican service in the chapel this afternoon."

He looked down at the sleeping baby.

"God bless you both," he murmured softly, and went out.

My heart sank.

My own chaplain had been round, or rather the curate had breezed in to say hallo and congratulate me, but he was young and just married and I didn't feel that he would understand what was going on inside me any more than I did.

Half past two found me sitting alone at the back of the tiny chapel and, as the short service began, so did my tears, cascading from brimming eyes and bouncing off on to my dressing-gown. I bowed my head, unable to sing, unable to do anything but sit there whilst the reservoirs inside me emptied. I don't remember much about the service and when it ended I hurried away, not wanting to speak to anyone, anxious to be back in my room and repair my face before the family arrived. But they were already there, at least the two older boys were, standing looking embarrassed and awkward not knowing what to do or say.

My room was on the ground floor; Jacques, my husband, was outside in the courtyard with Yves and Bee who were too young to be allowed in, and as I crossed to the window he lifted Yves up to speak to me. But my three-year-old son was petulant.

"I want to come in and see my baby brother," he pouted.

"So do I," chimed in ten-year-old Bee, her skinny brown plaits bobbing up and down as she jumped against the window-pane trying to see inside.

"*Why* can't I come in?" Yves wailed, his blue eyes angry and perplexed. "If Olivier and Hervé can see him, why can't I?"

"I'll bring the baby to the window," I cut in and, going towards the cot, picked him up and put him in Olivier's arms.

"There you are," I said, "hold him up so that they can see him."

But at fifteen Olivier was at the age when most things embarrassed him and having a baby thrust into his arms probably embarrassed him more than anything else.

"Here," he said, dropping the bundle onto his younger brother. "You take him."

I remembered Olivier gazing in awe into Yves' cot only three years earlier and the wonder on his face as I placed the baby in his arms. But time had passed and he had changed and was now in the full throes of adolescence.

Hervé went to the window and held Christopher up for the younger ones to see.

Bee stood on tiptoe, her brown eyes sparkling. I remember

thinking that she needed a haircut, her fringe was almost in her eyes.

Yves struggled in Jacques' arms.

"I want to kiss Mummy," he cried pathetically.

"I'll soon be home darling," I soothed, my face pressed against the window-pane.

"I want you *now*," he said and, digging his chubby fists into his eyes, began to cry.

At that my eyes filled once again, and I turned away. I could see that my husband's patience was wearing thin. Olivier and Hervé were obviously longing to leave, yet didn't quite know how to make their getaway.

"I think it would be better if you went and helped Daddy," I said, taking the baby from Hervé, "he seems to be having trouble with Yves."

They looked relieved, kissed me hurriedly and left.

I remained sitting on the bed with Christopher in my arms and once again the tears began to flow; there didn't seem to be any way to stop them. The day dragged on and just when the hospital was settling down to its evening routine the sister came in. She was small and plump and Scottish with twinkling china-blue eyes but as she sat down on the bed she looked at me intently and her face was serious and concerned.

"We'd like you to see one of the doctors before you go home," she began.

I looked up in surprise.

"But I see them every day," I answered.

"Not this one," she continued, taking a deep breath. "I think he'd be able to help you."

"Oh, I'll be all right once I'm home," I answered.

"We want to make sure of that," she ended. "I've asked Dr Dufour to pop in, he'll be here tomorrow at three."

"But *why*?" I enquired. "Who is he?"

The Sister took another deep breath.

"A psychiatrist."

I looked at her in alarm.

"Oh no," I cried, "I don't need a psychiatrist. I'm just a bit tired, that's all."

"It's more than that," she said quietly.

And, patting my hand, she got up and left.

I picked up my hand-mirror from the bedside locker and gazed into it. I looked awful. Where was the young mother's radiance?

"You're not a young mother," something inside me said. "You're nearly forty."

"That's probably it," I sighed as I put the mirror down and settled back against the pillows. But I felt momentarily reassured, it was at least an explanation.

Dr Dufour looked like a teddy bear, small and dumpy with hair sticking out of his ears. He came into the room, sat by the bed, held my hand and grunted. And I cried. We didn't get very far. All I remember him saying was, "I'm here, don't worry, I'm here". But I was worried about everything and the fact that he was there didn't help me at all. I suppose I talked to him, I don't remember, but he wrote out a long prescription and said he'd like to see me in a month.

Two days later I walked thankfully down the hospital steps, one hand tucked gratefully under Jacques' arm, Yves, talking non-stop, clutching tightly to the other. Fourteen-year-old Hervé was carefully carrying the baby, his dark head bent reverently over that tiny bundle who was to grow up to resemble him not only physically but in character as well. But, at seven days old, Christopher was just a plump, Eskimo-like creature with the wide-set almond-shaped eyes and the soft dark hair so characteristic of Jacques' family.

As I left the hospital behind me and walked out into the damp November morning I remember thinking, "Now all will be well, it's over and I'm going home." But everything was far from well.

Jacques bought the prescribed pills and I put them aside. He reminded me of my appointment with Dr Dufour, but I cancelled it. Sometimes after my return home there were moments when life seemed good, when I appreciated the children, the fun of them, the joy of having them around, but mostly I woke up in the morning to a flatness, a greyness and the day seemed to be an endless expanse of desert which, somehow, I had to cross in order to earn the oblivion of another night's sleep. And I went mechanically through each week turning deeper and deeper into myself. I was thirty-nine years old and what no one had told me was that the years were beginning to take their toll. I couldn't carry on in the way I had always done, and it hurt my pride and the image I had created for myself. I didn't want to admit that my youth was now behind me, that I was entering the dreaded "middle age" and self-pity, that most devastating of all human emotions, insidiously crept in and overpowered me, blinding me to everything else.

There were now five children of widely differing ages to be looked after and, more importantly, loved and I tended to forget that most of the time. Jacques, at forty-four, was at the peak of his career and very busy, the house was old and large and needed renovating and I hadn't married a handy man; all the work had to be done by professionals and there just wasn't enough money for everything. But I had joined the "me" brigade and wanted instant everything and the whole lot got on top of me.

Instead of staying quietly at home and taking things one at a time, I let the media convince me that I was a second-class citizen, that I needed to fulfil myself. So I rushed around to tea-parties, coffee mornings, meetings – to anything, in fact, which would get me out of the house. And Jacques, obviously worried about me, tried to cheer me up by taking me out in the evenings, with the result that life became a vicious circle. Because I was tired I became more and more depressed, and because I was depressed, I tired myself out running away from the things which I thought depressed me.

When I married Jacques he had a broken marriage behind him and three young children. And like so many people, I had imagined that a "friendly" divorce does not affect the children, that they would slip as easily into this new relationship as if they were going down a slide at the playground. But they didn't. Although they had only been two, six and seven when the marriage broke up, they did remember, at least the boys did, and what I was to learn the hard way was that no one can ever replace a mother in a child's life and heart.

I tried to do so, and I failed. I loved the three of them and they loved me and had I left it at that all would probably have been well, but I wanted more; I wanted to cut their years with their mother right out of their lives and make them mine and it wasn't possible, or even healthy.

The stupid thing was that I liked Jacques' first wife; in

other circumstances we could have been good friends, but between being good friends and becoming enemies was a whole strip of land and I raced across it and planted my flag.

Looking back I realise that, like Jacques, all their mother wanted was the best for the children, and she was even prepared to share them with me, but I wanted exclusive rights: it had to be all or nothing at all. And it almost ended up in being nothing at all. It was only when my own children arrived that I began to learn something about unselfish love and the deep ties which bind a child to its mother and remorse, that most futile of human emotions, set in. And then I almost went overboard trying to bind the five of them together into a family, forcing them to "love" one another. It was so unnecessary. They wanted to love their little brothers; they did love them. Their mother was the first to send me a congratulatory telegram when each one arrived. There was no animosity except in my mind and I almost ruined everything with my obsession. And the obsession fed the depression.

I now realise that many more women than we are willing to admit go through varying phases of "puerperal depression", and no one who has not experienced it can understand the depths of suffering to which one can descend. There doesn't seem to be any medical explanation as to why an otherwise "normal" woman, looking forward to having her baby, should be so afflicted after giving birth.

I'd heard about "baby blues" – an understatement to say the least. I'd experienced them first when Yves was born, and I took it that they must be a normal part of childbirth which I had to accept. So I accepted it and waited until the black cloud lifted which, after about six months, it did.

But with Christopher the depression was deeper and darker; I was mentally ill and needed help. But I refused to admit it and struggled on. In the end, the anxiety, the terrible overwhelming fear that "something would happen to the baby", the fatigue and the broken nights took their toll. Six months after Christopher's birth I ended up in a mental hospital with a breakdown.

For my soul is full of trouble… I am counted among those who go down to the pit.
(Psalm 88: 3–4) (New International Version)

2

ALONG WITH THE MADDING CROWD

The clinic I was sent to was outside Paris, so few friends visited me. It *was* a long way to come but I don't think that was the only reason. I think they were afraid, a breakdown was something they couldn't quite understand. An appendicitis, a hernia, a kidney operation, a heart attack or a thyroidectomy, these things are tangible, within everybody's comprehension, but a mental illness, at least in the mid-sixties, was still a very hush-hush affair and people didn't want to know.

The Anglican vicar and his wife came and also the laughing Scottish sister who had been so concerned for me when Christopher was born. How I blessed them for their visits. It gave me a feeling of normality again and I knew that there was a world outside those walls. But apart from Jacques and Geoffrey, my brother, who raced over from Germany where he and his family were stationed at the time, they were my only visitors and time hung heavily. And yet I had many friends, many real, loving friends, but perhaps in similar circumstances I would have been the same.

The first time I was in the clinic it was summer. The sun terrace was delightful and the patients sat on it for hour after hour: some smoked, some flicked through magazines, others idled or dozed or gazed into space. No one did anything useful or fruitful or creative and yet I am sure we were all, basically, creative people. It wasn't that the staff discouraged us, sometimes I had the feeling that they didn't even care. We were the means by which they earned their living but they would have preferred to have managed without us. We were a nuisance, rather like the cat who is put firmly out of the front door at night and no one bothers overmuch what happens to it until the next morning, when it is let in again. We were encouraged to leave our rooms as soon as we were allowed up, and there their responsibility ended.

I think the most difficult thing to bear in a mental illness is the loneliness, the feeling of isolation. How many times in the past years had I dreamed of having a day off, a day to myself, time which I could call my own without the incessant clamour of the family. Every mother does. And yet once I was up and about I had what I had always wanted, "time to be myself", and I didn't like it at all. There I was with a room of my own, meals brought on a tray, beautiful grounds to walk in, a sun terrace to sit on, and I hated every minute of it. Had I been in a hospital ward it might have been easier to face reality, but there in that dream world I felt completely cut off from the everyday things of life.

Not that I was alone. The "hotel" was full of people like me but we were each shut up in our own world, often a fantasy world, and had virtually no contact with one another. And yet what most of us needed was to be taken out of ourselves, not pushed further down inside. I knew nearly all the other patients by sight; we were a mixed group, men and women, and yet it was as if each one was caged around with barbed wire. No one made the initial effort to break the ice and so, in spite of the sunshine outside, the ice inside us remained.

I remember one beautiful sunny day being allowed out to go for a walk and, wandering into the local village, found myself in its tiny medieval church. It was empty and cool and I knelt there in the dim half-light. I had no idea why, it certainly wasn't my habit, but I went back again the next afternoon and the next and it became a part of my daily routine. I don't think I said anything, yet as I knelt there in the cool and the peace with the faint heady smell of incense all around me, memories of the early years of our marriage came pouring into my mind and I wondered where all that happiness had vanished to. It did occur to me that I could pray about it, but spontaneous prayers had never been my habit. In fact, I didn't pray at all except in church on Sunday or with Bee and Yves at night before they went to sleep and then it was only set prayers or a quick SOS sent up when there was a crisis in the family.

I was a nominal Christian, an Anglican, an active churchgoer, a member of the Ladies' Guild and on the electoral roll. All my life I had dutifully attended morning service but, after a flash of spiritual enthusiasm in my teens, it had slumbered into a duty or, at best, a social occasion. If anyone had told me then that prayer could be a lifeline, something one cannot live without, I wouldn't have believed them.

Jacques was born a Catholic but had fallen away in his late teens. Yet the Lord sometimes has a strange way of bringing his plan into action in our lives and with my husband his mother was the channel.

She had died from a sudden heart attack in the spring of 1961.

My mother-in-law was a lovely person and a very dear friend and help to me. Her death had been a dreadful shock to us all. We had been laughing and talking with her only minutes before it happened. In the unreal days before the funeral, in my own sorrow I wanted to comfort my husband, but I was surprised and puzzled by his lack of emotion. Jacques is not what everyone imagines a typical Frenchman to be; he is in fact quite the reverse, reserved and unemotional. I am the "up and down" one in our partnership. I don't know quite what reaction I expected from him – perhaps not a flood of tears but something, some demonstration of grief. But it was he who comforted me and, although deeply shocked and hurt, he was a pillar of strength to us all.

At the funeral service the Protestant pastor chose for his text verses from John 14, "My peace I give you . . .", because he said those words so typified Jacques' mother. He was right. Like her son, she was a quiet, gentle person and there had always been a tranquillity abut her, a kindness and selflessness which I had taken for granted. And now Jacques seemed to be upheld and strengthened, borne along on her sea of inner peace.

After it was over my husband and I went for a walk. We lived near the Bois de Boulogne and it was early June, the loveliest time of the year in Paris, and we wandered up and down those shady, leafy alleys beneath the lime trees and chatted.

"Don't you want to cry?" I remember asking him. "I know how much your mother meant to you. It's not normal to be so calm."

The children and I had cried bitterly.

He didn't reply immediately, as if he were seeking the right words.

"It's strange," he said at last, "but I feel her very near me, nearer in fact than she's been for a long time. Lately I've been busy and not seen that much of her, but now I feel her presence everywhere. And... I know that wherever she is, she's happy."

He shook his head almost in disbelief.

"That letter she left my father and me saying that she was not afraid because she was going home to be with her Lord," he went on. "I don't know what to make of it. It's almost as if she knew she was going to die."

We neither of us spoke. That letter had deeply affected us. And I think that was the beginning of my husband's walk towards Jesus.

In the August we moved out of Paris to our house in this lovely village of Marly-le-Roi, and a year later, in September 1962, my first child and Jacques' third son was born, Yves-Michel. I was sorry my mother-in-law hadn't lived to see our new addition to the family. She would have loved this sturdy blond baby with the plump rosy cheeks and big blue eyes.

Jacques had been very pensive that summer. I thought it was just the after-effects of his mother's sudden death or the shock of becoming a country-dweller after forty years, his lifetime in fact, as a Parisian, and I didn't take much notice. But in the autumn, when life had settled down again, he contacted the local Protestant pastor and began attending instruction classes and, a month after Christopher was born, my husband was accepted into the Protestant Church. In his usual quiet way he mentioned the fact to me, but I had become very involved in the many activities of the Anglican church in Versailles. At that time these were mostly social and although I considered Jacques' change of spiritual direction a "good thing" I didn't think it necessary for me to be there to share this public stand with him. So my husband went alone to make the most important step in his life, his decision to accept Christ as his Saviour and to live by his Word. And, as he drew nearer to Jesus, my mounting depression drove me farther away.

As I knelt there in the dim half-light of that old stone church that summer afternoon and all these memories came gently back, washing through my tired brain, I knew that my husband prayed: and a strange feeling of peace crept over me when I remembered this. Maybe that was the beginning of my long climb back to health and normality. I don't know.

On one of his early visits to the clinic when I had been

almost too comatosed to notice him sitting there by my bed, Jacques had left a Bible on the locker. I hadn't commented on this and neither had he. I hadn't opened it either, but that first afternoon when I returned from my walk and wandered aimlessly into my room, I picked it up and thought that perhaps I ought to read it. I'd heard somewhere that one should read a chapter a day, so that evening I turned to the Gospel of John. It was more a healthy exercise than anything else, a kind of marathon I set myself as I'd also been told that, in this way, one could read the Bible from cover to cover in five years. And the idea of casually letting drop at the church sewing party that I'd read the Bible in its entirety appealed to my ego.

So I dutifully tried, racing through my chapter each evening before thankfully putting it aside and plunging into the current novel on my bedside table. And, not surprisingly, I got nothing out of it. It was just words, and dry words at that. Like cleaning my teeth, my Bible reading became a habit I automatically performed every night and dispensed with as quickly as possible.

If only someone, a Christian, had come to me then and told me to stop running away, to sit still and count my blessings. I had so many. If only I had been shown that what was wrong with me was that I needed Jesus, I was not chronically mentally ill. But no one did. My church friends were sympathetic but I wonder if they knew the solution to my problem, if they knew that Jesus is the great healer, the only true psychiatrist. Maybe they had not met him themselves and, like me, were merely going through the Christian motions.

When I left the clinic I was "better", but it was an illusion – I was only better because I was rattling with pills. It's an easy solution to stuff your patients with medication and send them out to face the world, but it's not an answer, and it wasn't an answer for me. Within four months, just a week after Christopher's first birthday, I was back again in that luxurious prison which was bleeding my husband down to the last centime; and I began to despair.

Don't be afraid or discouraged, for I, the Lord your God, am with you wherever you go.
(Joshua 1: 9) (Good News Bible)

3

COME AND SEE

After Christopher was born, I had been told that I should not have any more children but all the medication I had been taking over the past months had completely upset my system and masked any symptoms or warning signs, until a test taken in mid-December, when I had insisted on leaving the clinic and returning home to prepare for Christmas, showed that I was over two months pregnant.

It would be difficult to describe my feelings at that time. Having babies had not been easy for me, each child had been a miracle and, as their wet, squealing bodies were placed in my arms, a feeling of wonder such as I have never experienced at any other time surged through me. I remember saying to Jacques after Yves' long, difficult birth: "No man, no matter what he achieves, can ever know the joy and satisfaction a woman feels when she holds her baby in her arms for the first time." I loved children and longed for another baby, but I was very frightened of what the outcome might be.

Dr Dufour, when hurriedly consulted, stopped all drugs and said curtly: "Get rid of it." But I had long since ceased to listen, much less be impressed by anything he said. We appealed to the head of the clinic who merely said: "If she has another child she'll be locked up for life; there's only a ten-per-cent chance that she'll be normal." And he advised me to go to England where "it was easy". Nobody wanted to know. I had always wanted a large family and I had been blessed with one. I was also convinced that abortion was wrong, was murder, in fact, and a terrible battle now began inside me between my longing to hold another baby in my arms and my fear as to what might happen if I did.

Christmas that year was a miserable affair. As far as I can

remember, I kept bursting into tears. Jacques was obviously very worried, but he also tried to put himself in my shoes and, after endless inward battles, he merely said: "If you really want to go through with this, then go ahead and have the baby – we'll manage somehow."

In desperation I rang the vicar. He and his wife had been so kind and understanding when they had visited me in the clinic and he was an older man with an almost grown-up family, surely he could give me the answer. He came round immediately and was very gentle, but his first words were: "If you were my wife, knowing what you've gone through, I wouldn't hesitate. You must think of the five children who are depending on you; what will happen to them if you lose your reason completely?"

I didn't know. And so I went to England to the hospital in London where I had trained as a nurse and, contrary to what the psychiatrist at the clinic had said, it was not "easy". The doctors were kind, sympathetic and helpful but it was by no means abortion on demand. I had with me my case history from the clinic and letters from the French psychiatrists and my gynaecologist, but I still had to see three of the hospital's psychiatrists before a decision could be taken. Mercifully, one of the consultants had been a young houseman at the hospital when I was in training and we laughed together and recalled the endless cups of cocoa I had made him in the ward kitchen in the early hours of the morning when I had been on night duty and he had been called out to a patient. I didn't know that he had later specialised in psychiatry and it was such a joy to find this link from my past: meeting him again enabled me to relax and so release the mounting tension inside me, making the whole nerve-racking business much less fraught. I'll never forget his last words to me before he met with his two colleagues to make a final decision:

"I think, knowing your case history, it would be best if we went ahead and terminated this pregnancy, but the decision is yours and only yours, and if you decide to keep the baby then we will do everything we can to help you afterwards."

His advice was like a gentle shower of rain falling on the parched earth after the heat of the day and I was very tempted to go ahead and take my chance. But how could they help me afterwards? There were twenty-two miles of Channel between us; my home was in France with my husband and family, not here in London. I went away and thought about it for a few days. I decided there was no choice.

By another strange coincidence, the sister in charge of the small ward into which I was admitted was a girl who had arrived at the hospital's Preliminary Training School on the same day as I had. We had worked and lived together for four years. What a blessing at such a time to have Judy with me. She was a born nurse and I had always admired her gentleness and her faith; and she hadn't changed. The night before the operation she sat by my bed chatting about old times, soothing and reassuring me, and three days later, pale and weak, with dark circles under my eyes, I went back home.

It was early January and the whole merry-go-round started up again. Added to the depression I now had a terrible feeling of guilt for what I had done and it seemed that everywhere I looked a finger was pointing accusingly at me. Every time I opened a newspaper or a magazine, I found an article on the horrors of abortion, pictures showing a two-to-three-month-old foetus, descriptions of how it was extracted from the womb, debates on whether the unborn child suffered, whether it could be considered a human being. On and on it went until I nearly went out of my mind with guilt and remorse.

Over and over again I told myself that I had had no choice, that countless doctors, even my vicar, had strongly advised me to go ahead because of the consequences of another birth. And yet, deep down inside me, I knew that I *had* had a choice, that in spite of what anyone said the final decision was mine and mine alone. No one could have removed that little baby which was growing in my body had I not given my consent; and my life became a constant nightmare from which I could find no avenue of escape. In my nominal Christianity, I believed that God was punishing me. It was only later when I came to know him that I realised that he doesn't punish us; by flouting his laws we punish ourselves. He forgives us, but sometimes we find it hard to forgive ourselves and carry the scar with us for the rest of our lives.

Jacques was at his wit's end and I should imagine his financial end too, though he never said so, and by mid-January I was ready to go back into that clinic again. I didn't want to go, but I didn't want to stay at home either; I was at peace nowhere. We were at a crossroads and each fork seemed to have a no entry sign up.

It was then that a friend, more an acquaintance really, said that if I would throw away my pills, which had been prescribed again, she and her prayer group would pray for me. And I was so desperate I clutched at this last straw.

My husband agreed to let me do it, providing he could stay at home from the office to look after me. I don't know what he was afraid of, perhaps that without the support of drugs I would succumb and take my life or murder the children, I don't know. I was half-crazy with medication and could quite easily have done either. But something seemed to tell me that his fears were unjustified as, with great trepidation, I threw boxes of wildly expensive drugs down the lavatory and flushed them away. And these women began to pray. I am sure Jacques did too, perhaps even I did, I can't remember. I had become so turned in on myself that if I prayed it was doubtless a selfish prayer, a "me" prayer. But I slept that night and I got through the next day and the next. I won't say that it was easy and I'm not suggesting that everyone with a breakdown does the same. I think it depends on how close Jesus is to coming into your life and, although I didn't know it then, he wasn't far away.

Gradually I learned to live with my situation, in a pretty neurotic way, but I picked up the pieces and carried on and I didn't go under. There were grey days and black days and very few bright ones, certainly no golden ones until that dreary morning at the end of February when Claire, the friend who had prayed, rang and asked me to go with her to a women's retreat the following day.

"There's an incredible speaker," she enthused, "who's come over specially from Switzerland... I'm sure you'd enjoy hearing her."

"Claire," I protested, "it's not really my thing."

Nothing was. Life was still like a deep grey sea stretching endlessly and menacingly towards a black horizon.

"Come and see," she pleaded. "I'll call for you at nine thirty."

And she hung up.

I liked Claire and I was grateful for her group of friends who had and, as far as I knew, were still praying for me, but she was a bit too way out for my liking, and she always seemed happy. It was abnormal.

"Oh well," I shrugged as I turned away from the telephone, "why not? I can always ring her in the morning and say I can't make it."

But when the morning came for some reason I didn't, and when promptly at nine thirty Claire knocked at the door, I was there waiting with a strange feeling of expectancy – and I didn't know why.

She smiled her wonderfully radiant smile which started in her deep grey eyes and quickly spread over her face like ripples breaking the sunlit surface of a still pool. Her name, which means "brightness" or "light" in French, suited her admirably. She was small and trim and everything about her had a shining transparency, a bubbling joy which was infectious. Her soft brown hair bobbed up and down as she walked and I had to hurry to keep up with the racy spring in her step.

"So glad you could come," she said as she started the car. "We only have these special speakers twice a year and they're really not to be missed."

I mumbled something in reply as she weaved in and out of the traffic, wondering why I had come. Claire looked round at me as if she read my thoughts and her small hand reached out and rested for an instant on mine.

"Relax," she smiled, pulling into a wide driveway, "I'm sure you're going to enjoy it."

Her enthusiasm was contagious yet, that afternoon when the meeting ended, I turned to her unconvinced.

"Claire," I said abruptly as the chairs scraped back across the polished floor and about a hundred women prepared to leave the hall, "all this really doesn't apply to me; it's too fanatical."

The speaker that afternoon, a tall, grey-haired Swiss woman with a radiant face, had talked about being a "committed Christian" and having a personal relationship with Jesus Christ. And although I had been a churchgoer all my life, I had felt distinctly uncomfortable.

Claire looked at me searchingly.

"I don't think we're fanatical enough," she replied quietly.

I glanced up and her steady gaze disturbed me; she had that same radiance as the speaker.

"Oh Claire," I began and I laughed awkwardly as my sentence tailed lamely away.

But the hall was rapidly clearing and, at this stage, the clatter of tea cups in the next room was more appealing to me than a religious discussion.

As we entered the dining-room, I had no difficulty picking out the "good churchgoers"; we seemed to stand out like hatpins. The others, those committed Christians, had a freshness, an openness, a warmth and a genuine friendliness which I hadn't seen before in a church crowd. Their faces reflected an inner serenity and, like Claire, they seemed to be always smiling as if they really enjoyed life, indeed the whole business of living. As I accepted a cup of tea and turned back into the relaxed, chattering crowd, a feeling close to envy crept over me.

These women were talking about Jesus as if he were their next-door neighbour. I hadn't pronounced the name since I was five, dutifully lisping prayers at my bedside every evening; it seemed slightly indecent to be so openly familiar with the Creator of the Universe. God, or at the limit Christ, was permissible in everyday conversation but Jesus... No!

"Oh, there you are."

Claire was back at my side with the elegant woman who had introduced the speaker.

"I'd like you to meet Patricia," she smiled. "She's got five children of all ages... just like you."

I couldn't believe it. Patricia was tall and slim. The soft, clinging, oatmeal-coloured wool dress she was wearing showed off her figure to perfection and the mass of flame-coloured hair piled high upon her head looked as if it had taken hours to arrange.

She held out her hand and as her smile spread across her face it lit up eyes of a deep sapphire blue. There it was again, that radiance.

"We've just been talking about starting a Bible Study one afternoon next week," Claire went on. "Will you come?"

I felt cornered: she hadn't said, "Would you be *able* to come", but, point-blank, "Would you *come*?" Almost as if the decision were already taken.

"I'm pretty tied up..." I hesitated.

"I know you are," Claire continued warmly, "just like Patricia is, but I think you'd enjoy it, we're going to do a series called 'The New Life'. Is any afternoon better than another for you? We haven't made a choice yet."

This time I felt really trapped.

But "The New Life"; it sounded tempting, not the sort of thing I expected from a Bible Study. Just what I was longing for, in fact, a new life with wings on, flying away from all those dishes, those nappies, that pile of ironing, the all-enveloping depression.

"Well," I hesitated again... and was lost.

"How about Monday?" said Patricia. "No one does anything on a Monday afternoon and it's good to get out of the house. On Tuesday the debris never seems quite so bad."

She laughed and fine, feathery lines crinkled round those shining eyes.

"I'll pick you up about one thirty," Claire broke in before I had a chance to reply.

I said nothing. I still felt trapped but in a nice, safe way and, anyway, why not? I wanted whatever it was so many of these women had; I wanted a smile which didn't look like an advertisement for toothpaste, put on for the occasion; I wanted the genuine love and joy I saw in their faces.

The crowd was beginning to thin.

"Let's go," said Claire, taking my arm, "we don't want to get caught up in the Friday evening traffic."

And with a wave to those who were still standing around chatting, she steered me towards the door.

I needed steering.

I was still convinced that the meeting was not for me, yet I felt as if a heavy, dragging weight had been lifted from my shoulders and I had suddenly become airborne. And the feeling was delightful. I didn't realise it then, but this was what those other women had which I so envied, that freedom which comes when a heavy burden is removed. Only they weren't being steered by Claire, but by this Jesus they talked so easily about.

Come and see what God has done... Come and listen... let me tell you what he has done for me.
(Psalm 66: 5/16) (New International Version)

4

THE ENCOUNTER

Monday morning found me once again in the grip of despondency. The weekend had been a total disaster familywise; Jacques had been away for three days and returned home tired and far from pleased to find a list of things which had gone wrong in his absence and which needed attention. Homework had either not been done or left until the last minute, Yves had had tantrums most of Sunday and Christopher had cried all night with ear-ache.

I awoke on Monday morning physically and mentally exhausted to hear rain slashing down on to the roof and dripping from the gutters along the side of the house. There was only one thing I wanted to do, turn over and sleep for a week or, better still, fall into oblivion and forget that I had ever been born. But the alarm clock was relentless.

"You forgot to mend my track suit and I've got gym this morning," accused Hervé, coming into the kitchen half-dressed, trailing a torn track suit behind him.

Hervé, at fifteen, was still the laziest, untidiest, dirtiest creature I had ever come across. He never washed unless pressurised and everything he wore was always in shreds.

"Why didn't you remind me?" I muttered, taking the track suit and looking despairingly at the great rent in the leg. "I can't be expected to keep tabs on *everything* you tear to bits."

"I *did*," he answered hotly, and grabbed the offending garment back out of my hands, an angry glint in his eyes.

How like his father he looks, I thought, except that Jacques was rarely angry.

"I'll borrow Olivier's," he threw over his shoulder as he stormed out of the kitchen.

"No you *won't*," said his meticulous elder brother as they collided in the doorway. "I'm fed up with you taking my things and giving them back filthy and in bits."

"Heaven help me," I groaned, "it's going to be one of those days."

And I turned appealingly to Olivier.

"Can't you lend him your track suit," I pleaded, "just this once?"

"It's always just this once and it's always the same," he exploded angrily. "Oh, all right, but tell him to give me back my physics book. He borrowed it last night and now he says he can't find it."

I wasn't surprised. It needed a pitchfork even to get into Hervé's room, let alone find anything.

"Here," I said in exasperation, "stir these eggs and I'll go and have a look."

Olivier was always bad-tempered in the morning and the least thing which went wrong became a major calamity.

"I don't *want* to go to school," wailed Yves.

On and on it went.

"Where's Shirley?" I asked desperately, lacing shoes, brushing hair, finding books, calming the hungry baby and burning toast all at the same time.

"Shirley's got a headache," said Bee, her now bobbed head appearing round the kitchen door. "She's not getting up this morning but she'd like a cup of tea when you have time."

Shirley was the au pair and she often had a headache – especially on Monday mornings.

"She's got a hope," I muttered. "Here, Bee, just put Chrissie in his highchair while I finish the toast, and pour Yves' milk for him before he spills it all over the table."

Thank heaven for that little girl, I thought, she's always so sweet-tempered.

"I want to pour it *myself*," yelled Yves. "And I'm *not* going to school."

"Oh yes you are," I answered grimly, snatching the milk jug and taking his mug firmly from his hand.

"Everybody happy?" said Jacques imperturbably, coming in to the general chaos.

Christopher picked up his baby dish and jammed it upside down on his head, porridge trickling into his eyes and running down his face.

He seemed delighted.

"*Look* what he's done," wailed Bee, "*all* over my drawing."

And she burst into tears.

"But why did you put your drawing near him?" I snapped. "You know what he's like."

"You told me to look after him," she sobbed.

I snatched the book and began wiping splodges of porridge from a highly-coloured illustration of the middle ear.

"I *wish* you children wouldn't leave your homework till the last minute," I snapped again.

"But last night you told me to go to bed and finish it in the morning."

I could see the whole situation was getting on Jacques' nerves.

"Must fly," he said, pushing back his chair on his half-eaten breakfast. "Don't forget to ring the builder about that missing tile on the roof, oh . . . and you'd better put a bucket at the top of the stairs till he comes. With this rain, anything could happen."

"Anything *else*?" I flung sarcastically as I removed the baby and chair into the kitchen for cleaning.

My husband sighed loudly and, ruffling his daughter's hair, bent to kiss her.

"Don't cry, darling," he soothed. "I'll bring you a little surprise tonight to make up for the drawing."

Bee stopped crying immediately.

Jacques poked his head round the kitchen door on his way out.

"Don't wait dinner for me this evening," he called blowing a kiss in my direction. "I've got a meeting which could go on till all hours."

"That's the story of my life," I shouted after him, "waiting for you."

But the front door slammed and he was gone.

The dining-room was beginning to clear as one after another they found books, gloves, marbles, pencil cases, bus passes and assembled for the day's battle.

"Can someone see Yves across the road?" I called. "His school bus will be here in a few minutes and Christopher's not dressed; I can't leave him alone."

"Oh ... *no*," came a chorus. "We're already late."

And with a final clatter they were gone.

"I'm not *going* to school," menaced Yves and he looked at me defiantly.

"Oh well, *don't*," I snapped and immediately regretted it, knowing full well that in a matter of minutes he would too. And he did. It was then the phone rang.

"It'll be about a quarter to two when I get to you," said Claire brightly. "I'm *so* looking forward to it and I'm sure you'll enjoy it. Bye."

And she rang off before I had time to tell her I'd changed my mind; the black clouds were there all around me and I simply couldn't face it. I dialled her number, but it was engaged, so I went to take Christopher out of his high chair then tried again, but it was still engaged.

"Oh well," I shrugged, "I'll give her a ring at lunchtime. She's going anyway, so it won't make any difference to her."

But at lunchtime there was no reply and at one forty-five there she was on the doorstep, small and vivacious and impeccably dressed, smiling that wonderfully sweet smile of hers.

There didn't seem to be any reason why I shouldn't go. Shirley was up, though groaning: she was a lively little Londoner who had come to France as an au pair to "better herself" and avoid, as she so often told me, "the life my mum had". She was the eldest of a large family who had obviously been brought up with a rod of iron, and she made no secret of the fact that she thoroughly disapproved of my more lenient pedagogic methods. But Yves, the real thorn in her flesh, had gone meekly off to school, Christopher was at last asleep, the house still looked like a disaster area ... but I went. This new life intrigued me ... and especially those women who had what I wanted.

The following Monday I went again and the week after that, and gradually, as the women in the group, many of them the "churchgoers" I had picked out at the first meeting, got to know and trust each other, they opened up and began to share their problems.

But I still sat on the fringe.

I still couldn't say "Jesus" as if he were someone other than in a stained-glass window and I didn't pray out loud as most of the other "churchgoers" were hesistantly beginning to do. In fact, I didn't pray at all except the conventional prayers in church on Sunday, or a desperate plea when a child had a temperature or Jacques was on the road and hours late. But I no longer felt embarrassed. I even began to look forward to those Monday afternoon meetings. Something inside me was beginning to thaw, to melt away after all those years of putting Jesus into a box and leaving him safely up there on the altar, only to be approached at Holy Communion. I was beginning to catch some of the joy, the love and the hope of those other women, and yet I knew that their lives were not always easy. Most of them had problems, some of them seemingly insurmountable.

One whom I remembered from that first meeting had been abandoned by her husband to bring up six children alone; the youngest was only three and sometimes came with his mother to the meetings. She had sat apart that first Monday afternoon, as bewildered as I was, and yet now she was changing, the bitter lines had gone from around her mouth, her whole expression had softened and she had a new serenity which I envied. Another had lost her forty-five-year-old husband through a rapid cancer and a third told us of her teenage daughter who was hooked on heroin.

But I think the woman who made the deepest impression on me was the one who led the Bible Study. Three years earlier, just as he was about to leave for university, her only son had been killed in a car accident and, although she told me that she had "cried buckets" since, she radiated that elusive something I so longed to have; that deep, unshakeable inner peace and hope and the conviction that death is not the end but the beginning. And Jesus was very real in her daily life.

As week followed week, an occasional ray of sunshine gradually began to pierce through those enveloping black clouds and words from a chorus we'd so often sung at the Monday meetings rang from time to time in my fuddled brain: "He touched me, he touched me and oh the joy that filled my soul. Something happened and now I know he touched me and made me whole."

He had touched me and something was indeed happening in my life and, although I didn't know it at the time, God's plan for me was unfolding. Jesus had been digging and hoeing the rough soil of my heart long before I realised it and now he was removing the stones and preparing the ground ready to plant his seed of love. He was about to come and take over the garden of my heart, the mess and chaos of my life and, when he did, he gently took me back down the years and healed the scars the psychiatrists had been unable to close as he showed me that real love, his love, does not seek to possess, but to give. And that he loved me just as I was. And when that happened I was able to open up the deep recesses of myself to him, to drop the mask and accept myself as I was with my fears, my obsessions, my insecurities and my anger.

"Do you know Jesus?" Patricia asked me one spring afternoon.

I looked away and the answer must have been obvious to her.

"If you ask him," she continued gently, "he will come into your heart and be your personal Saviour. You can have a relationship with him just as you have with your earthly father. You don't need flowery language or set speeches, you just have to believe that he died on the cross for your sins, that he rose again and is alive in the world now. Do you believe that?"

Still I didn't answer.

Like so many people, I wasn't aware that I was a sinner. I felt more sinned against.

"You don't have to tell me," she ended. "Just tell him that you want him to take charge of your life, that you are willing to relinquish the reins and follow him along the path he has chosen for you. He has a perfect plan for each one of our lives if only we are willing to follow it, and it's when we don't and go our own way that things go wrong," she ended quietly.

The Bible Study was over and the others were already chatting in the dining-room.

"Come and have tea," said Patricia, getting up.

But it wasn't tea I needed; I had come to the end of myself but at the end of the tunnel a bright light was shining, beckoning me.

"I must go," I muttered, "I'm in rather a hurry today."

Patricia said nothing, but walked with me to the door.

"God be with you," she said softly, as she stood on the step beside me.

I think she knew what was in my heart.

There was a battle raging inside me as I drove through the quiet streets and into the country road which led to my own home – the battle every faithful churchgoer fights when he comes face to face with the living Christ and knows that going through the motions every Sunday, however earnestly, is no longer enough.

I knew that after all these years of trying, of being "someone" in the church, of organising, doing, being, that I was doing it all in my own strength and for the wrong reasons. For my glory and not for his.

I also knew that the time had arrived when I had to come down on one side of the fence or the other. That I could go on "doing" and "being" in my own strength, or I could capitulate, acknowledge my need, my weakness, my utter worthlessness, confess myself as the sinner I now knew myself to be and accept his cleansing love, receive his gift of eternal life and have that joy and peace which I'd so envied in those born-again Christians.

I pulled the car into the side of the road and stopped the engine. It was May and everything around me was singing with the first awakening of trees and buds; the afternoon sun was slanting westwards and I shielded my eyes as I turned and looked hopelessly across a stretch of lawn speckled with daisies.

"I can't face going back to the chaos," I said out loud. "That endless round of dirty nappies, children fighting, an au pair who has merely added her problems to my toppling pile, and a husband who is always working. I'm so tired."

Tears of self-pity began to roll down my cheeks. I was tired, it's true, but I was also very sorry for myself. I picked up the Bible on the seat beside me and idly flicked the pages as the tears continued to flow. It wasn't even my Bible. My own King James' Version which I'd received at my confirmation years before had been sitting collecting dust in the bookcase ever since. No, this was a new modern version which one of the group had lent me and I noticed that she had underlined verses here and there.

"Come to me and I will give you rest – all of you who work so hard beneath a heavy yoke," stared up at me.

"Rest," I echoed wearily, "rest from the endless round of chores. Will you give me that rest, Lord?"

There was no response, and I don't think I even expected one. Then, suddenly, my eyes fell on a verse from Isaiah which had been heavily underlined.

"Seek the Lord while you can find him. Call upon him now while he is near."

And it was as if a voice said:

"I know your limitations. I don't expect you to do something you cannot do. I only ask you to come to me and take me as your Saviour, then I can carry your burden and use you for the work I've planned for you to do. The work that only you can do for me."

At that moment I felt that Jesus was very close. I felt very special and precious to him, as it dawned on me that he had chosen me for a certain task as he chooses each one of his children and I stopped calling him "God" and *hoping* he'd heard. For the first time I called him "Father" and I was *sure* that he heard.

That little spark of faith which had only been big enough to hope now suddenly flamed into a fire and I knew for certain that Jesus was alive, that he wanted to be my friend, my counsellor, my Lord and my Saviour. But, above all, that he wanted to make my heart his home.

And I invited him in.

"Jesus," I whispered, as the tears ran steadily down my face, "I believe you died for me, that you would have suffered that terrible death on the cross if it had only been for me, and I want to ask your forgiveness for doubting you all these years, for playing at being a Christian without your cleansing and your power in my heart. But today I surrender completely to you all I have, my time, my talents, my life. They're yours anyway; you gave them to me. Now I want to live in your will, your strength, your love, I want to have your peace and your joy. Help me, Father, always to remember that you are alive and at work in me from now on and let me never again try to do anything in my own strength, but only through you."

As I looked up, the tears were still flowing freely, but the

grass seemed greener, the daisies bigger, the sky bluer;
everything had taken on a new dimension, a deeper hue. I
was aware, as never before, of the beauty of God's creation
all around me and as I drank it in a deep peace began to flow
through me, cleansing me, filling me, wiping away years of
anger, resentment, bitterness.

I knew that externally nothing had changed, the dirty
nappies, the unwashed dishes, the quarrelling children and
the broken nights were still here. But, inwardly, I now had
that certainty, that peace, that precious fellowship with
Jesus and I trusted him completely for my future and my life.

I turned the key in the ignition and the car began to slowly
move on down the hill.

There was a sudden rumble, then a screeching of brakes
and a yelled curse as a swaying lorry, full of sand, shot out of
an open gate and ran straight into the side of the car.

*You should not be surprised at my saying, "You must be
born again".*
(John 3: 7) (New International Version)

5

AND SOMETHING HAPPENED

The man who stepped down from the lorry was stocky, thickset and menacing; his untidy grey hair showed flecks of vivid red and his complexion matched the flecks. As he stamped in my direction, fists clenched at his sides, he looked like a maddened bull charging to attack. But I didn't feel afraid; the new me sat calmly by the steering wheel and, to my surprise, smiled.

This appeared to enrage him beyond all control and, as his face darkened with every step he took towards me, abuse and recriminations spat from his mouth. His fellow-worker, who should have been guiding him out of the garden and into the narrow roadway, appeared sheepishly from behind the lorry but, seeing that I wasn't reacting to the violence, quickly joined the driver in hurling accusations. And, as the two of them clotted together in a united front, I opened the door and got out.

The accident was entirely their fault, driving into the road without warning yet, for some reason, I seemed to be unconcerned about the fact that I was being wrongly accused and abused. I looked down at the great dent in the rear door and grimaced as I realised how nearly they had missed me and, instantly, under my breath, I murmured, "Thank you, Father", before turning to wait for the storm to abate.

This wasn't at all like me and for a moment I felt stunned. I seemed to be walking around on a theatre set, moving in and out of a situation like a character in a play; acting a part which was the opposite of the person I was in real life. Normally, I would have been first in the fray, giving as good as I received and the whole thing would have disintegrated into a sordid squabble. But not today.

As I stood there, I saw our family doctor, through whose

front gate the lorry had burst, come out of the house and down the path towards us.

"I'm so sorry about this," he said as he reached my side. "I've just finished afternoon surgery and am afraid I didn't see what happened."

He looked accusingly at the two workmen and they both began to shout at once, but the doctor cut them short.

"You'd better send for your boss," he said firmly, and they subsided.

But the boss had been warned and was already running down the driveway. He was the builder who had done some of the renovations to our old house two years before and, looking from the doctor to me, was obviously keen to keep the peace with both his customers. His two workmen looked furtively at each other.

"I think the best thing would be for you to come and see my husband this evening," I said quietly. "He'll be home after seven."

And getting back into the car I rolled slowly down the hill.

As I pulled up in front of our house the door was flung open and Hervé appeared closely followed by Yves, a large slice of bread and jam in his hands.

"*Please* Yves," I said for the umpteenth time that week, "*don't* wander about whilst you're eating. Sit at the table."

As usual, he took absolutely no notice, merely made a dive at my legs and caught me in a jammy bear hug. Then he saw the car.

"Hervé," he yelled to his brother, "quick, come here. Look what Mummy's done to Daddy's car."

Immediately the old spirit of resentment began to boil up inside me. Why was it always "Daddy's car" – never mine? But as quickly as it had arisen, the feeling evaporated, and I was able to see the situation through Yves' eyes. Jacques always drove when we were together so, to a four-year-old mind, it was natural that it should be "Daddy's car"; and again I wondered at the new me. I couldn't believe that that simple act of faith, those few words telling Jesus I wanted him in my life, that I was sick of myself and especially my tongue and I wanted him to take charge, had brought about such a miracle. I had peace. This car collision was the evidence.

I playfully smacked Yves' rump and he looked up at me, a mischievous grin on his face.

Hervé was slowly walking round the car.

"Bet you gave them a mouthful," he whistled. "Wish I'd been there, don't you Olivier?"

His elder brother had just come out of the house.

"What happened?" he enquired sympathetically. "Are you sure you're all right?"

Olivier, at sixteen, could be extraordinarily sweet and understanding at a time of crisis.

"Oh, I'm perfectly all right," I smiled. "It's just the car. The builder's lorry charged out of the doctor's garden straight into me."

"Don't you wish you'd been there?" Hervé said again. "Bet the sparks flew in every direction."

I looked up at them all standing admiring my dented car.

"As a matter of fact," I replied evenly, "they didn't. Not on my side at least."

Three pairs of eyes swivelled towards me in surprise.

"I've changed," I ended quietly.

The two elder boys looked at me enquiringly.

At the Bible Studies we had been told that when we met Jesus and gave our lives into his hands it was important to tell someone immediately, in a way to seal the bargain, but also to be a living reminder to ourselves that we believed this precious new life had begun and we had been born again. But would the children understand? Weren't they too young? So I said nothing and the moment went by.

I realise now that age has nothing to do with it and the children would have understood perhaps better than anyone else, but I was afraid of ridicule and I didn't want them to know that I had surrendered everything into someone else's hands, that my life was no longer my own. After all, we had faithfully marched to church every Sunday as a family and, up till now, no one had ever told me about this new life; this personal relationship with Jesus. And, immediately, doubts began to creep in. Had I imagined it all?

But the feeling of happiness and peace was beautiful and I didn't want it to stop, so I pushed the queries out of my mind.

"Come on boys," I said brightly, "let's go in before Yves daubs everything with jam. Is there any tea left in the pot?

I'm dying for a cup."

As we went up the steps to the house, a wriggling, squealing Yves now firmly imprisoned in Olivier's grasp, Bee appeared round the kitchen door.

"Daddy rang," she announced.

I looked at her heart-shaped face and lustrous, velvety brown eyes and understood, for the first time, why her father had likened her to a baby deer and nicknamed her "Bibiche" long before she could even walk. I had shortened it to Bee and rarely called her Marie-France, the name by which she had been christened.

"Did he want anything special?" I enquired.

"No," she replied, "only to say he'll be home early."

And taking Yves by the hand she skipped off with him into the garden.

I went into the kitchen wondering what my husband would think when he saw the car; I knew I could rely on Yves to rush at him with this choice titbit the minute he set foot in the house.

Christopher banged his spoon delightedly on the tray of his highchair and held out his chubby arms when he saw me. I picked him up before I sat down to pour out some tea from the rapidly cooling pot and as I slowly sipped the tepid brew he snuggled against me, warm and cuddly. I could hear Yves and Bee laughing together on the garden swing and suddenly I saw my life as if it were passing on a screen before my eyes.

On one side were the positive aspects, on the other the negative ones and, as I mentally checked them off, I realised how many blessings I really had. The children became Jesus' gifts to me, precious gifts to be loved and brought up for him; mine but above all, first and foremost, Christ's. It was wonderful, I could love and enjoy them, but from now on he was in charge. I could hand over these precious burdens and receive my orders: all he asked was that I should take time to be with him, to talk to him, to listen to him and to worship him.

That wonderful extra dimension, that heightened colour and awareness which I had first experienced sitting in the car in the roadway came back and I felt again that surge of peace which had flooded through me just before the lorry came hurtling out of the doctor's gate. I realised it had never left me, in spite of the collision, and it was like the feeling I had had in hospital after being given pethidine to quieten the contractions before Christopher was born. Then I had floated in space, the pain gone, relaxed and completely at peace, but the feeling had only lasted the time it took for the drug to wear off, then the pain had returned. Now I knew that this sensation was something permanent, it was Jesus' peace, a peace I could count on for the rest of my life as long as I kept my eyes on my Saviour and didn't let the angry, mountainous waves of life close over my head.

And I marvelled not only at the change in me, but at the speed of the change. Only a few weeks ago, Jesus had still been a plaster figure in a church or part of a stained-glass window, and the Bible a book to be kept on show in the bookcase but rarely taken down. Now I suddenly had a gnawing hunger for his Word, because I had found Jesus as a real presence. Tears of joy, tinged with sadness, spilled over onto my baby's curly head at the realisation of the wasted years I'd spent trying to cope without him.

Christopher stirred and looked up at me. His violet-blue eyes searched mine then he put up a podgy hand and his baby fingers stroked my face as he pursed his lips and forced himself upwards.

"Kiss, Mummy," he lisped.

I realised that he was puzzled: in his little mind, tears were associated with pain and yet he could see that I was smiling and he couldn't understand. Hugging him tightly to me, I bent and kissed his soft, warm cheek and, reassured, he slipped off my knee, staggering and finally collapsing into his favourite play-pen, the dog's basket.

I sat on in a dream. And it was as I sat staring vacuously into space that I began to see myself as God must see me, and I realised that all these years I had fooled myself by imagining that thinking beautiful thoughts, and there hadn't been many of those lately, and doing good deeds was enough. That these things somehow covered up the pride, the selfishness, bad temper, resentment, jealousy, self-pity, all the rubbish which had accumulated in and cluttered up my heart for so long.

And in that moment, they all marched before me in a dreadful pageant, those insidious sins, and I was able to stare at my life, my now dead life, aware that for the first time I was really seeing myself as God had seen me all along. And I knew that by myself I was incapable of changing anything, that only God could wipe away those sins and turn them into ashes. I now knew for certain that I *had* experienced that new birth; all things had truly become new and I was a new creature in Christ. My old self had been crucified with him and I was now resurrected with him into his life.

I also knew that I had to tell someone and Claire was the obvious person. I went upstairs into the bedroom and picked up the receiver; there was a click and I heard her voice at the other end of the line and, suddenly, I didn't know what to say.

"It's ... me," I began lamely and no more words came.

But Claire understood.

"Something's happened to you, hasn't it?" she said gently.

"Yes," I replied, and could get no further.

There was a pause when we each waited for the other to speak.

"Thank you for telling me," she went on quietly, breaking the silence. "I've been praying for this."

Then the tension broke.

"But I haven't told you *anything*," I laughed.

Claire laughed too.

"You didn't have to," she replied. "As soon as you spoke I knew you'd met Jesus. Praise the Lord."

"Praise the Lord," I echoed, and realised that I'd said it spontaneously, and for the first time.

I put down the receiver and looked through the window at the children playing in the garden below. The sky was the colour of a tea rose and the pink and white blossom sprayed upon the cherry tree was stretching up to meet it; and I saw the beauty of the old grey stone walls encircling my home, the graceful sweep of the weeping willow whose leaves were dusting the lawn. As I watched, Yves raced out, laughing, from beneath its shade, closely followed by Bee; she grabbed hold of his flapping shirt triumphantly shouted "Tig" and raced back beneath the drooping boughs.

Almost hysterical with laughter, Yves skidded round to follow her, then suddenly stopped and with a shriek of "Daddy" tore off to the other end of the garden to where his father had just come through the heavy wooden street door.

My heart seemed to expand and burst within me as I turned from the window and walked down the stairs to join in the noisy greetings of children and the excited barking of dogs in the hall below. And for the second time that afternoon I was aware of my many blessings.

Jacques looked up from their midst and smiled his enquiring, half-amused smile. And I knew he'd seen the car.

"I'm sorry," I said lamely, sitting down on the hall settle.

"It's only *things*," he said quietly, disentangling himself. "As long as you're all right, that's all that matters."

He came over and kissed my cheek.

"What happened?" he enquired, sitting down beside me.

"The builder's lorry," I answered. 'He's coming to see you about it any minute now."

My husband looked at me thoughtfully.

"Are you *sure* you're all right?" he ventured. "You seem different."

He paused.

"You're not worrying about the car, are you?"

"No," I replied hesitantly, "no, it's not the car."

The children had disappeared again and the dogs had returned to their baskets. The hall was dark and cool and peaceful as my husband put his hand over mine.

"Then what *is* it?" he asked gently.

He waited, but I didn't reply: the words jammed in my throat. Then I heard the rattle of the builder's lorry as it drew up in front of the house and I knew this wasn't the time, this change in my life was too important to throw out as a casual remark over my shoulder. I wanted to tell my husband when we were alone together, quietly.

He got up and as I rose to follow him to where the builder was waiting, my whole being seemed to be singing and I realised that for the first time in years I was really looking forward to tomorrow.

Therefore, if anyone is in Christ, he is a new creation; the old has gone, the new has come!
(2 Corinthians 5: 17) (New International Version)

6

FROM A LONG WAY OFF

I awoke very early next morning with a feeling of freshness. The house was still and although Jacques stirred he did not wake as I slipped out of bed and crept past the doors behind which the children were peacefully sleeping and on down the stairs into the drawing-room.

On a table near the window my Bible was lying where I had left it the previous afternoon and, sinking into an armchair, I leant forward and picked it up. I still didn't know my way around the pages but, as I held it in my hands and idly flicked, it fell open of its own accord once again to the Book of Isaiah, chapter forty-three, and suddenly the eighteenth verse stood out from the rest of the page.

"But the Lord says, 'Do not cling to events of the past or dwell on what happened long ago. Watch for the new thing I am going to do. It is happening already – you can see it now.'"

The words leapt out at me, pricked my eyes and danced with life and meaning as I sat there motionless, unused to the stillness, the new peace and, most of all, bewildered and thrilled by the reality of the words on the page before me. I felt that never again would I read the Bible as a duty. Now I longed for more and knew that I needed to delve deeper into God's Word in order to get my spiritual food and nourishment and my pattern for this new life.

The dogs barked sharply and I heard the splutter of the grocer's van starting up. It must be six o'clock, the time he always left for the market to collect fresh fruit and vegetables for his general store next door, and I knew that I had nearly an hour before the house would stir and the "busyness" of the day begin.

I slipped to my knees and laid my head against the chintz-covered arm of the chair.

"Loving Heavenly Father," I heard myself saying and then no more words came, but it didn't seem to matter, I was lost in love and adoration for this Father who had suddenly become so real to me. And as I knelt in silence with waves of peace and joy flowing over me, my soul reached upwards to worship my Maker and I knew that words were not important; that, at times, they were almost a hindrance. And I marvelled again at the sudden miraculous change which had taken place in me. I was living in an age where everything was "instant" from coffee down to airline tickets, everything had to happen in the twinkling of an eye, but I had never expected that the tired, disillusioned self-pitying woman I had been only yesterday morning could, through that one act of surrender, emerge as a new person with a purpose, a future, with hope – a woman who had found peace. And yet it was so.

I don't know how long I remained kneeling, but it must have been for half an hour, a half-hour I shall never forget as, so often since, I have been unable to recapture the fourth dimension I experienced that morning. During my later prayer times, I have often felt it necessary to keep up a one-way conversation with God, reciting my "shopping list" of requests, telling the Lord what I wanted him to do and how he should be running the world. But not on that pearly Tuesday morning. That was my baptism of fire when I felt the touch of his hand on my life and his Holy Spirit pour over and through me.

Suddenly, as if from a long way off, almost from another planet, there was a small hand shaking my shoulder. I looked up. Yves in his bright blue teddybear pyjamas was standing barefoot at my side.

"When's breakfast?" he asked matter-of-factly. "I'm hungry."

I turned round and hugged him.

"Not until you're dressed."

He scampered back upstairs and as I followed him I heard Christopher's cooing and incomprehensible jargon. The day had really begun, but the memory of those moments of quiet, of peace, of communing with Jesus had impressed themselves deeply upon me.

Jacques came sleepily out of the bedroom door and

blinked short-sightedly when he saw me.

"Where on *earth* have you been?" he yawned.

I kissed his cheek and ran before him into the bathroom. He was more bewildered than ever. I have never been a "morning person". Getting me to bed at night has always been a problem and getting me out of bed in the morning an even worse one, yet here I was skipping around like a young fawn and it wasn't even seven a.m.

I began to sing to myself as I quickly dressed then went to pick up Christopher who was standing in his cot watching Yves shoot cars across the bedroom floor.

"Don't forget, no breakfast till you're dressed Yves," I called over my shoulder as I left the room.

The house was beginning to stir and I hurried; I wanted this, the first day of my new life, to start properly. Even if homework wasn't finished, shoes were lost and there was the usual mad scramble to catch the bus, I didn't want to be caught up in it. I wanted to be there as the bastion, the focal point, but a smiling good-tempered focal point, a happy mother the children could remember as they raced out of the house: and one they wanted to come back to.

"Help me, Lord," I breathed as I went into the kitchen, settled Christopher in his highchair and tied an apron round my waist. "This is really the worst moment of my day, help me to remember that it's you who is in control, and no longer me."

And I began to sing again as I cracked eggs into a basin.

Jacques appeared in the kitchen door and came over to where I was standing. He put his arm round my shoulder and kissed my cheek.

"I don't know what's happened to you," he said quietly, "but I like it."

He waited, but I didn't say anything.

"Perhaps some time you'll tell me about it," he said gently, and turned away.

I nodded, my heart too full to speak. And I remembered Jacques' remark of the evening before – that I seemed different. So it *had* been true. If my husband had immediately noticed that something was changed, it wasn't my imagination; and once again I sent up a fervent prayer of thanks.

The children were beginning to clatter down the stairs and, as usual, Yves was in everyone's way and coming in for a great deal of backchat. As I picked up the jug of hot milk and went to the table, Jacques was bending down listening to something Bee was earnestly telling him. The boys were already attacking the cereals and as I sat down and began to pour out coffee my heart continued to sing.

"Got a busy day?" asked Jacques, looking up as he held out his cup.

"Not really," I smiled.

"Any chance of your meeting me for lunch?" he queried.

For a moment I paused, the old me struggling for survival. It would have been so satisfying to make a cutting remark and bring out how tired I was, how overworked, how with all these children could I possibly... but the new me won the battle and I smiled.

"If it's not too early I'd love to," I replied. "Shirley should be back before twelve thirty and she can take over. By the way, where *is* Shirley?" I ended.

"Expect she's overslept again," said Bee, slipping out of her chair. "I'll go and see."

Bee was a born peacemaker, always anxious to avoid trouble for everyone.

"Yes, do," I called after her, "tell her her egg is getting cold."

"Nobody said anything but I could feel their eyes on me. Shirley liked getting up about as much as I did and her frequent late appearances at breakfast usually drove me into a frenzy. They all knew how badly I reacted to my own worst trait in Shirley, but this morning I saw my au pair through my own eyes and sympathised with her problem.

Jacques pushed back his chair and got up.

"I'll give you a ring about eleven," he said, "to see how things are going and then you can tell me what time we can meet."

I could see that he wasn't at all sure that the early morning euphoria would continue into the day.

"Lovely," I replied. "I'll look forward to it."

My husband gave me a searching look and left. I think he understood this tremendous thing which had happened in my life and knew it was something too deep to throw out as an aside over the breakfast table.

The dining-room was beginning to empty and, as the children collected up their things for the day and left, Shirley came quietly into the room and slid into her chair as unobtrusively as she could, obviously expecting a blast. But none came.

"You will be back by a quarter past twelve, won't you?" I asked her. "I'd like to go into Paris for lunch."

She gulped, totally abashed by the lack of outburst on my part.

"Yes, of course," she stammered.

"Good," I answered. "I'm just running across to the bus stop with Yves. I won't be a minute. Keep an eye on Christopher for me; he's had his breakfast."

I took Yves' hand and we ran down the steps together.

It wasn't until later that I realised it must have been the first time in months he had caught the bus without protesting.

Peace I leave with you; my peace I give you. I do not give to you as the world gives.
(John 14: 27) (New International Version)

7

REVELATION

I got off the train and began to make my way through the crowded Paris streets to the restaurant. Spring seemed to have suddenly stopped and the cloudless blue sky of early morning had turned a leaden grey: thick, puffy clouds, black at the edges, hung menacingly and the gentle breeze which had swayed the cherry blossom was now beginning to whip through my light wool suit. People were hurrying to and fro, heads bent, eyes averted, everywhere the usual lunchtime crowd which I hadn't noticed before. I had once, no doubt, been a part of it. The song in my heart seemed muffled by the anxious, tense, unsmiling faces all around me; everyone seemed to be bent against an imaginary wind, scurrying like rabbits to their burrows, looking neither to right nor left. The occasional tourist loitered in front of a shop window but the office-bound Parisian appeared to be caught up in a web of his own making.

Had it always been like this, I wondered, or was it just today? But, apart from my inner joy, outwardly today was no different from any other day, and I realised that before I had been so taken up with myself and my own affairs that I had never had time to look around me, except in a disinterested, superficial way.

Each time I had come to Paris I had been in a hurry, and often bad-tempered, racing against the clock. If it had been an evening visit, I had invariably rushed out on homework unfinished, the baby not settled or Yves crying because I'd hurried through his bedtime story. And, having my priorities all wrong, I'd always ended up with a guilt complex on top of my irritation.

But today the Lord had also given me an extension of time. There seemed to be lots of it, floating about above my head like soft, fluffy clouds, instead of the black depression which had been hanging menacingly there for so long. And because of this new freedom, I was able to look with compassion on those people whom so recently I had mirrored, those tense, unsmiling faces hurrying past me.

Jesus was there with me that May morning, nursing his new-born child, and he helped me to see people through his eyes. He gave me a special insight into their hearts and lives, allowing me to pierce the mask and uncover the fear and hurt we all try to hide ... And for the most part I saw an emptiness which I had never dreamed existed.

I felt he was saying to me:

"Look at my people; your brothers and sisters. Yet they do not know me. They are being fooled by Satan into believing that the pursuit of happiness is all that matters, that materialism and false gods will bring them joy, that there is a way to peace which excludes the cross. But these are my flock, my sheep and yet they do not know their Shepherd. How can they recognise me unless you who have met me go out and tell them, bring them back home into the fold, into my harvest?"

And as I looked around, the harvest was so great it frightened me and I mentally recoiled from such a task. But Jesus said:

"Without me you can do nothing ... but with me all things are possible. Go out in your weakness and I will pour my strength into you."

But I had arrived at the restaurant in a quiet side-street and Jacques was waiting. He put down his newspaper as I came in and rose to meet me and I knew that God had not brought us together by accident, that we had a work to do for him and that in his power we would do it.

I slipped into the seat beside him and smiled and he smiled back. It seemed a long time since we had been so quietly and happily at ease with each other and I knew that a new life had begun not only for me as a person, but for us as a couple. As I studied the menu my heart was pounding, just as it had done when I was a young girl, out on a first date; there was that same feeling of expectancy inside me and I didn't know what would develop, what the outcome of our lunch would be.

As the waiters glided noiselessly between the tables, I sat

back against the red plush seat, lulled by the snatches of muted conversations which rose around me. The small restaurant was crowded and while Jacques gave the order I gazed idly around and noticed a honeymoon couple at the table next to ours. They were talking softly and endearingly to each other and as I watched the young wife put down her fork and lovingly fingered her shiny new wedding ring, looking up adoringly at her husband as she did so. They were so obviously in a world of their own that I felt embarrassed to be intruding even by glancing in their direction.

A voice broke into my day-dreaming.

"We have not seen you for a long time, Madame."

I looked up to see the manageress of the restaurant standing at my side.

"May I offer you an aperitif?" she enquired.

I smiled and shook my head.

I always liked the personal touch in this small, intimate restaurant. It had been Robespierre's house and the two small, low-ceilinged rooms were decorated throughout in deep red, with eighteenth-century prints hanging on the walls. Jacques often came here with business associates and although it was well known it was tucked away down a narrow alleyway and so was completely hidden except to those in the know.

We began to eat and I wondered how I was going to begin, how I was going to put into words this new life which had begun for me and for Jacques too, in a way. Throughout the meal we talked easily and effortlessly about everything and nothing. It wasn't that we were avoiding the subject which was uppermost in our minds, it was just that no explanation seemed necessary, and, as he ordered coffee, Jacques looked at me and smiled and I knew that he understood what had happened to me; that everything was clear and transparent between us. Those few words spoken in the kitchen before breakfast were just part of his Gallic diplomacy, his way of approaching and skirting round a subject rather than going straight to the point. He hadn't wanted to force me into saying something before I was ready and now that I was ready words were no longer necessary.

My husband had known that I was going with Claire to the Bible Studies and, like Claire, when my decision to

commit my life to Jesus had at last been made I didn't have to
tell him in so many words, he knew. And I marvelled, and
still do marvel, at the silent communication which exists
between Christians. It was something I had not come across
before but which, from that moment onwards, I was to
recognise whenever I met another totally-committed Christian brother or sister. There was a kind of telepathy between
us, an instant of recognition when we seemed to skip all the
preliminaries and immediately made contact.

I stirred my coffee thoughtfully.

"I'm sorry it took so long," I said at last.

Jacques leant across the table and took my hand.

"It was worth waiting for," he replied.

And we left it at that.

As we walked out of the restaurant and into the Rue du
Faubourg St Honoré, the sky seemed to have lifted and
spring had returned to Paris; the sun was breaking through,
round and dazzling, and the air was like champagne, soft
and gentle yet scintillating. We parted on the corner of the
street, Jacques to return to his office and me to make my way
leisurely back to the station. As I wandered back along the
tree-lined boulevards, I realised that it was a long time since I
had enjoyed being in Paris, since I had appreciated the
beauty of the city, since I had been positive, in fact. And in a
pensive mood I climbed into the train which was waiting to
take me back to that home I now saw through different eyes,
that home which from now on had Jesus at the helm.

*Come unto me, all ye that labour and are heavy laden, and
I will give you rest.
(Matthew 11: 28) (King James' Version)*

8

ACTION STATIONS

In the days and weeks which followed, I never ceased to marvel at this second chance which had been given me to become the wife and mother, the person I had always longed to be but had never been able to manage on my own.

Now every sense was sharpened. I had fallen in love with Jesus and he had taken me as his bride. I was in my honeymoon period and, like all brides, I imagined that this was how it was always going to be. Jesus was kind and loving and patient as a bridegroom and he led me gently through those halcyon days and, although I didn't realise it then, began preparing me for the valleys and rocky roads which would follow as, little by little, I learned that being a Christian is not an insurance policy against pain, that Christ does not take us out of the storms of life or shelter us from problems and tragedies, but he does give us his strong hand to hold and his peace in the midst of them.

Jesus had taken from me the selfish, possessive love which had dominated my relationships in the past and poured his agape love into me. I now realised that this had been Jacques' kind of love for some years and I had taken it for granted or, at times, even ridiculed it, thinking him weak to take my abuse and bad temper and other people's injustice and not retaliate. Now I knew that it had been Jesus working in him and producing that wonderful, unselfish love which my husband poured on his family and, indeed, on all those with whom he came into contact. And now that that same Jesus was giving me this kind of love, I saw my husband in a different light and a new depth of understanding was born between us. We walked together to face the future, confident that, although we did not know what the future held for us and our children, we *did* know who held the future. And, gradually, our family life began to change.

I realised that my role as a mother held a responsibility which, up till then, I had not accepted. That "mum" is the hub of the wheel round which all the spokes revolve and if the "hub" is off key, bad-tempered, sulky, unhappy, then all the spokes react accordingly and the atmosphere of the home is poisoned. Now, each morning, I gave my day to Jesus, knowing that alone I could not be the person he had always wanted me to be; asking him to fill me with his love, to see my family and everyone I came in contact with during the day through his eyes. And I always rose from my knees at peace, confident that I would be able to face whatever the day would bring. Those quiet moments with Jesus, saying good morning to him before saying good morning to my family, unlocked a flood of blessings and changed our family life in a way I had never dreamed possible.

It was a beautiful summer, warm, sunny, dry, and as day after day dawned on cloudless blue skies it didn't seem possible that life could ever have a care again. But although I did not know it at the time, Jesus was preparing me.

At the end of June, school finished and, as we were having major renovations done to our old house, we scattered the children in all directions. They were happy to go off to the seaside with relatives: Yves whooped with joy at the idea of going to stay with cousins in the South of France and my parents jumped at the chance of having the placid, easy-going Christopher to themselves for a few weeks. Her year's au pairing finished, Shirley went back to England and the footballer she'd pined for ever since she arrived. Calm settled over everything ... then the workmen moved in and hammered and sawed all through the heat of July.

Most of our local friends had gone away and, with the house like a bombed site, it was impossible to have visitors. It was, in fact, impossible to do anything at all as every room was either being attacked with pickaxes or else being used as a depository for the furniture which had been removed from the disaster areas. So, in the freshness of the early morning, I took my Bible and went to sit in the shade under the drooping branches of the weeping willow tree and remained there, oblivious of time or hunger, until the lengthening shadows on the lawn told me that I should think about picking my way through the debris inside and trying to scrape a meal together for my tired, home-coming husband.

Those weeks supplied a deep need inside me, a hunger to learn more of Jesus and his Word and, as I devoured the chapters, stopping from time to time to seek help from one of the numerous Bible commentaries I'd taken from the bookshelf in Jacques' study, a picture slowly began to form in my mind: a picture of life as Jesus wanted it to be, as God had always intended it to be from the time of creation, and I was able to look down at the ashes of my life, a life I no longer wanted, which had dropped from me and been burned in the fire of his love.

I also began to see that being a Christian carried a responsibility with it; it wasn't all cake and cherries. I knew now that I was saved, that eternal life was mine, not because I was better than anyone else but simply because I had accepted this precious gift, God's grace. And I felt humbled once more that Jesus, who cared so much, would have suffered and died that terrible death on the cross even had it been only for me. Understanding that, I also understood that Jesus hadn't died just so that I should bask in the sunshine of salvation, but that, knowing him, it was my duty to go out and share him, spread his Word to the hungry people around me who were lost and living in darkness.

I remembered how, as a teenager not long after my confirmation, I had wanted to become a missionary. I don't think I had a very clear idea of what a missionary was and it was war-time and all such dreams were permissible because there was no question of being asked to meet the challenge. But in those days, it had conjured up a picture in my mind of pygmies and topees and treks through steaming jungles, Bible in hand, and I suppose, romantically, I had thought how wonderful it would be. But without any real feeling of commitment.

Now, sitting in my sunny garden, I realised that perhaps then, when I was merely paying lip-service to him, God was already preparing me for what he wanted me to do, years later. And it dawned on me that one does not have to gallop half-way across the world to reach people for Jesus, one merely has to stretch out one's hand to those around. I saw again the hungry eyes and the tense, unsmiling faces of the

Parisian office workers scurrying along the busy boulevards, and knew it wasn't just chance that had brought me to Paris.

Again I marvelled at the way God ties up the loose ends and brings events in one's life round to a full circle. How many times in the past years, when things had gone wrong, had I blamed the fact that I had been uprooted, that I didn't fit in here? In fact, it had become quite a joke between Jacques and me – though I didn't always think it funny! Whenever things didn't go the way I wanted, he would say teasingly:

"Of course, I *know* such a thing would *never* have happened in England."

And I remembered the number of times I had flashed round with a biting remark, telling him that indeed it wouldn't! As if, on the other side of the Channel, sinks didn't get blocked, vacuum cleaners didn't groan to a stop, repair men always turned up when expected and children never got bad marks at school.

I had been so busy feeling sorry for myself, a poor "foreigner" in an alien world. Now it was as if God was saying to me, there in that beautiful French garden, that he had placed me here; that I had taken a long time to discover that and seek his will for my life and he had been willing to wait, but now it was time to start being positive and bloom where he had planted me, amongst a people he had given me for my own. And he pointed me to the Book of Ruth. I remembered having learned the poem "She stood breast high amidst the corn" when I was at school and it hadn't meant much to me, but as I opened the Bible and began to read her story, I knew that what Ruth had done I could do.

Jacques came home that evening to find the workmen gone, the house deserted and me still sitting in the shadow of the weeping willow, tears rolling down my face. When he wandered into the garden looking for me, I rushed at him, full of new resolutions and good intentions. He listened patiently to my outpourings and smiled his slow, wise smile, perhaps even then wary of my effusion.

"If you feel like that," he said gently, "if you're at last convinced that God has placed you here for a reason, it's no good crying. The best thing to do is make a plan of action."

Action has always been his motto; dreaming has been

mine. And now he was challenging me.

"Come on," he said, "the kitchen's in a worse mess than ever; there's no point in trying to make dinner, wash your face and I'll take you out. And let's put this plan into action, *now*."

He didn't add "before your enthusiasm wanes", but I knew he was thinking it.

That evening we sat at a table in the quiet cobbled street outside our local bistro and talked.

"I've always wanted to start a Bible Study group at home," Jacques said, "but I didn't feel you were ready for it and, anyway, with the children there always seemed to be so much to do in the evening. But if you feel that now is the time, let's get down to organising it."

And there and then we began to plan.

The group was to start as soon as the summer holidays were over and we decided it should be held every Monday evening.

"Patricia was right," Jacques said. "It's a good time. No one ever goes out on a Monday so the people who come should be able to make it regularly."

Faced with a *fait accompli* I began to draw back.

"But who will lead it?" I demurred.

Jacques looked at me, his hazel eyes behind his glasses were kind, almost laughing at me and my cowardice now that the crucial moment of truth had arrived.

He reached across the table and took my hand.

"The Holy Spirit," he answered quietly. "Who else?"

I breathed a sigh of relief, not really taking in what he had said, just grateful it didn't have to be me.

"But," he went on, "working through each one of us in turn. Would you like to begin?"

I quickly withdrew my hand.

"Oh *no*," I cried. "I *couldn't*."

Jacques said nothing for the moment, just looked at me steadily.

"You can and you will," he replied at last. "But with the Lord's help. Have you forgotten the words, 'Without me, you can do nothing, but with me all things are possible'?"

I didn't answer, I knew what he was hinting. Day after day I was reading, devouring the Bible, hungry for more; now my husband was challenging me to put into practice what I had learned.

"If the Lord has spoken to you," he went on, "through all those tense, hungry people you saw when we had lunch together in Paris, it was for a purpose. I have seen for a long time the masks behind which so many are hiding, but I knew that until you were willing there was not a great deal I could do about it from home. But now that we both recognise that we are surrounded by lonely, frightened people, it's a wonderful challenge to be able to go out and do something together."

I knew he was right and I recognised that, like my missionary dreams at fifteen, I was still at the fantasy stage and hadn't accepted the Lord's challenge with anything but my mind. Now God told me that he doesn't make mistakes, that I hadn't married Jacques by chance, that it was all part of his plan which was now opening up before me.

I also knew that it did not depend on me, that all I had to do was place myself in my Lord's hands, trust him completely, keep close to him through prayer and his Word as I had been doing during the past two months, and he would work through me and do the rest. The ultimate responsibility was not mine. All he asked me to do was sow the seeds; I wasn't responsible for the harvest. But if I refused to sow the seeds, if I kept my lips closed and didn't tell those around me what Jesus had done to change my life, when I met my Lord face to face I *would* be responsible for all those who, perhaps because of my silence, had not met Jesus.

"You're right," I said to my husband. "I'm willing to do whatever you want me to. Let's open our home as soon as school starts again and go on from there. I know God will make it clear just what it is he has in mind for us to do."

We left the restaurant arm in arm, a deep feeling of oneness and peace between us as we walked home together in the gathering summer dusk. At the top of the hill, a full moon was rising behind the spire of the Louis XIV church which dominates the village and, as we approached our home, it shone on the old grey stone walls surrounding the house, lighting a silver pathway to our door.

Words from childhood, long since forgotten, flooded my mind.

"God's in his heaven, all's right with the world."
And at that moment, all was truly right with my world.

You who bring good tidings to Zion go up on a high
mountain. You who bring good tidings to Jerusalem, lift
up your voice with a shout,
Lift it up, do not be afraid; say to the towns of Judah,
"Here is your God!"
(Isaiah 40: 9) (New International Version)

9

THE COUNTER ATTACK

July melted into August and we joined the children for long, lazy days on the sun-baked Mediterranean beaches which stretched around Narbonne, Jacques' family home. Then, as was our custom, packed them all into the car and went to finish our holiday in England.

Jacques' theory was that the soporific effect of sun-drenched days needed the sea breezes of the Essex coast afterwards in order to whip up everyone's circulation and set up the family for the gruelling school year ahead. And his theory seemed to work. The children arrived at their grandparents' home brown and relaxed for a couple weeks of unpredictable weather, mostly spent racing madly across wet sand or playing energetic games of cricket – their version – on the green behind our rented bathing hut, and the combination was perfect.

My euphoria continued during that holiday and yet, like most Christians, I found that a disrupted routine gives the devil a heyday. Somehow, prayers and Bible reading got pushed aside in the daily scramble of picnics to prepare, friends to be contacted and gear to be collected up and pitched into the car before driving off for another bracing day by the sea. In fact, I almost began to think I could manage very nicely, thank you, without Jesus, as the headiness continued even without my daily communion and delving into his Word. I assumed I was someone "special" in Jesus' plan, even a cut above other new-born Christians and think I must have become slightly condescending, if not pompous, in my "Christian" attitude – a sin which, as a mere "churchgoer", I had been spared.

Then one Sunday afternoon, towards the end of the holiday, we were lazily keeping our eyes on the bobbing forms of our children amongst the mass of others in the water below when the Salvation Army band began to play on the promenade.

I went down and sat on the sea wall below and Jacques joined me. We stayed for their service and once again I was struck by the lack of interest in Jesus and his message from the laughing crowds passing to and fro. It was a beautiful afternoon and some people stopped to listen, but very few; most of them just turned lazily over on their towels and barely reduced the volume of music blaring from their transistors.

My mother was sitting in the door of the beach hut, chatting with an old friend who had come over for the day. They were both active members of their local church ladies' guild and worked endlessly sewing and knitting for the various bazaars and even now, as they talked, their needles were clicking. Ever since I could remember, my mother had been busy in the church, had taken us to matins on Sunday morning and, when we were older, to evensong, had seen that we went to Sunday school and been confirmed. Yet, looking back, I was convinced that she had missed out on the peace and the joy, was a Christian in name only and had never really met Jesus.

Our holiday was rapidly drawing to a close, we were, in fact, due to leave for France two days later, so I determined to speak to her about it before we left.

But little did I realise that those holiday weeks when my precious moments with Jesus had been pushed to one side had caused a veil to be drawn over my relationship with him. I was now doing things in my own strength without first consulting my Lord, and the result turned out to be disastrous.

That warm Sunday evening we sat in my parents' twilit garden relaxed and at peace after a day in the sun, the smell of the lavender my mother had planted beneath the drawing-room window mingling with the scent of late cabbage roses. As the trees cast shadows on the lawn, I loosened my tongue and prepared to evangelise. But I attacked, there is no other word for it. From the height of my self-righteousness I attacked, and the moment I opened my mouth I put my foot in it.

My parents listened politely, even with interest, but I couldn't make them see that they were sinners and, looking back, I'm not surprised. People are going to react when bluntly informed that they are going to hell, especially when they have always followed the law and done everything they think they should according to church rules and, not unnaturally, they resented my pomposity. My father called me a fanatic and the subject was closed. He was right; I was a fanatic in the nastiest sense of the word and I had failed because I tried to operate in my own strength, not in God's. Instead of being loving and simply introducing them to Jesus, my Friend and Saviour, and telling them what meeting him had done to change my life, I attacked my parents' beliefs with a sledge hammer with the result that I shattered in a thousand pieces the faith I was trying to build up. I hadn't yet learned that the way to melt an iceberg is with warmth, not a pickaxe!

Yet the Lord is gracious and patient and so loving and he gave me a second chance, but it wasn't until many years later. Now he showed me that, although there is only one way to him, there are different ways of presenting him to others and I had not chosen the right one. It was my first lesson in humility and it took time to sink in; but I was learning.

And so we returned home, me still smarting over my parents' stubbornness to accept the wonderful gift "I" had offered them. "I" had come back into the foreground and a wall was gradually building up between Jesus and me, a wall of no communication.

The summer ended, school started again and life returned to normal. But not quite. I decided that the "new me" didn't need an au pair, I was going to manage everything myself and it was all going to be more wonderful than before.

Jacques didn't comment about this blaze of enthusiasm as together we sat down to plan our campaign for winning souls to Jesus and working for the Lord.

Our home Bible Studies started in October and already I was beginning to find time a problem with the many schedules and school deadlines to be respected, plus all the extra activities I had feverishly thrown myself into. In addition to the church choir, which I had enthusiastically taken over, I had also been elected to the PCC and the church social committee. Added to the numerous ladies' meetings and bazaars I'd volunteered to work for, there was not a lot of time left over for Jesus... And the dark mornings were quite different from those soft, dewy dawns when the sky was full of opal tints and the curtains stirred gently as a scented breeze drifted in through the open window. Then bird song twittering in and out of the foamy blossom had beckoned me to rise and worship. Then all pointed to the romantic side of Christianity and the romantic in me had responded, drinking deeply at the beauty of God's creation.

But now dark, cold mornings and a heavy staleness in the drawing-room atmosphere didn't beckon me in quite the same way. I found that I was making excuses, telling Jesus how hard it was (as if he who had spent long days ministering and yet had gone out before dawn to seek his father and pray, didn't know!) to get up when I was so tired, when I had such a busy day ahead of me, so much to do . . . and all for him! Little by little I fell back into the old pattern of scrambling out of bed at the last minute and racing round in a panic with everybody late. And, as I did so, my time with Jesus began to be shorter and shorter.

I found myself muttering prayers as I washed the breakfast dishes, telling myself it didn't matter where I prayed, the important thing was to pray. I hurried through other chores and managed to squeeze in the odd request or two as I went. And, all the time, I was fooling myself into believing that I was so busy doing God's work, throwing myself whole-heartedly into different activities for him, driving myself into a frenzy so that lost souls should come to him, that he would surely understand, he knew how unselfish my motives were, that if I had the time I'd spend it with him as I used to, I'd quietly read and drink in his Word, but for the moment all the other activities crowded him out and he couldn't but be pleased.

But he wasn't. And he didn't understand. And, gradually, as my scrappy prayer life became a grocery list or a timetable of things which I needed him to do, he began to be not so close and the world crowded in once more.

Then a new face appeared on the scene, someone I hadn't met properly before. Satan!

I'd read about him in the Bible, and loathed him, but the personal demon who was assigned to me wasn't so easily recognisable; he was a likeable chap who wished me no harm at all. He even wanted the best for me. *His* best. All I had to do was keep looking the way I was looking, away from Jesus, and everything was fine. I discovered that the devil was really very understanding. He didn't mind if I called myself a Christian, he didn't mind if I went to church, I could even read my Bible if I had time, but he saw to it that that was in even shorter supply, and he comforted me when I had a guilty twinge about my shrinking spirituality. Then he would confirm what I had been telling myself ever since I started building that wall between Jesus and me, that I was doing God's work and he'd understand. And I believed him! So the devil encouraged me to get busier and busier, whispering that as I was working for the Lord, the Lord would help me. What he didn't mention was that the Lord *he* worked for wasn't the one I had met face to face, but it took me some time to discover that.

Yet, occasionally, I'd remember those summer days when I had walked hand in hand with my bridegroom and I would long for that peace in the midst of my self-imposed whirl, long to kneel down in adoration and talk to Jesus. And it was then that Satan revealed his true colours!

I could do anything but pray, because then he knew he'd lost me. He could watch me read the Bible and even point out confusing passages to me, sow doubts in my mind. He could quote and twist it, that didn't bother him, he knew the Bible ten times better than I did, better probably than anyone who has ever lived. But prayer was a direct line between myself and my Maker, and no matter how hard Satan tried, he couldn't break in, he was powerless. Then he would fly into a terrible rage and all the venom in his black heart would come hurtling out in a volcanic rush if ever I managed more than a hasty SOS to Jesus over the sink.

What had happened to that fourth dimension?

But I was so busy I didn't have time to ask myself. The telephone rang constantly with meetings, discussions, things to organise, bazaars to work for and I fooled myself into believing that this was what God wanted from me.

But it wasn't. And he went farther and farther away.

Your enemy, the devil, prowls around like a roaring lion looking for someone to devour. Resist him, standing firm in the faith, because you know that your brothers throughout the world are undergoing the same kind of sufferings. (I Peter 5: 8/9) (New International Version)

10

AN EMPTY PILL BOX

One Monday evening towards the end of winter, Bible Study in our home had just ended, Jacques was putting the car away and I was collecting the coffee cups littered around the drawing-room when the phone rang. I glanced at the clock; a quarter to twelve, who on earth could be calling at this time? And immediately panic thoughts of my family in England flashed through my mind. Something dreadful must have happened!

"I'm sorry to bother you, but I didn't know what to do."

The voice at the other end of the line was distraught, but far from winging across the Channel, came from a very short distance away.

It was Paul, a friend of the boys, whose mother was also my friend. He was fifteen and his voice was at that stage when he couldn't entirely control it, but the break in it now was not purely vocal. There was deep, genuine fear and pent-up emotion.

"Paul,' I said urgently. "What on earth's the matter?"

He gulped, fighting to gain control.

"It's Mum," he said blankly.

"Yes, but what?" I insisted.

"Nickie just found her... unconscious."

He stopped, obviously finding it difficult to go on.

"We think she's taken something," he ended hoarsely.

"Are you *sure*?" I gasped.

There was no response from the other end of the phone.

"How do you know?" I coaxed. "Are you sure she's not just sleeping heavily?"

Anne also had five children and must sometimes feel as worn out as I did.

"No," he whispered, "there are boxes of pills, empty ones,

all around the bed ... and we can't rouse her."

"I'm ringing for an ambulance immediately," I said, trying to keep my voice calm. "Pick up all the boxes and wait. We'll be round immediately."

And I ran out into the cold night air shouting to Jacques to get the car out again.

At that hour it didn't take us long to eat up the few kilometres which separated the Grangers' house from ours but, even so, as we turned into their road an ambulance flashed past us and I caught a glimpse of a hunched figure sitting at the back.

"It must be Paul," I said. "That'll be the ambulance I rang for. Let's follow it, he'll need us."

"Some hopes of following it," Jacques said grimly, as we saw the white car with its blue light flashing on the roof already far into the distance.

"Well, go to the hospital then," I snapped.

Jacques stopped the car.

"*Which* hospital?" he asked patiently. "There are at least three to which they could have taken her. The most sensible thing is to go to the house and find out how Nickie's coping."

I collapsed. As usual, he was right.

The house was quiet when we arrived. Nickie was still up, looking stunned, and as we entered a child upstairs began to whimper plaintively.

"I'll cope with her," Nickie said automatically. "Please go to the hospital and stay with Paul. They've taken her to St Germain."

I could sense he feared the worst and looked at him in amazement, marvelling at the composure of this thirteen-year-old who, suddenly, had assumed such maturity.

"You can ring me any time," Nickie said as we left. "I'll sleep in Mum's room, the phone's by the bed, then I'll hear if Sophie cries."

Sophie was now crying very loudly and Nickie ran up the stairs two at a time to comfort his little sister.

It never occurred to either of us to ask where his father was. Charles travelled a great deal and I suppose we assumed he was away on business.

When we arrived at the hospital, Paul was sitting alone in the deserted out-patients' department, a sleepy night porter his only companion. As he rose to meet us my heart went out to him. His young face looked tired and haggard, and his curly blond hair was untidy and dishevelled.

I hugged him and he crumpled in my arms.

"What happened?" I asked softly as we sat down on either side of him on the hard bench.

"I don't know," he answered blankly. "Nickie and I had been to the cinema and when we got home he went to tell Mum we were back. The light was in the bedroom so we thought she was reading; but when Nick spoke to her she didn't answer, so he went over to the bed and she was lying there without moving. We tried to shake her, but she just flopped back."

He gulped and stared down at his hands clenched tightly between his legs.

"It was then we saw the boxes on the floor and we didn't know what to do, so I phoned you," he ended hoarsely.

"You did right, Paul," I said soothingly. "Where is she now?"

"I don't know," he replied blankly. "They rushed her off behind that door."

He jerked his head in the direction of a swing door marked "No admittance". I looked at Jacques and he got up.

"I'll go and see if I can find something out," he said quietly and disappeared down one of the endless corridors.

Up till then shock had numbed me, but slowly questions were beginning to form in my mind.

"Paul," I said gently, "have you any idea why your mother should have done such a thing?"

He didn't answer immediately, but swallowed hard, a battle of loyalty obviously waging in his mind.

I waited.

"It's Dad," he blurted out at last, without looking up.

This was the first time he'd mentioned his father and the pattern of unasked questions gradually started to fit into place.

"What about him?" I pressed.

I had seen Charles come off the train on Friday evening as I waited in the car for Jacques, and he'd waved cheerily in my direction before leaping into his bus as it started to move away.

"He's left," Paul said abruptly, still gazing intently at the floor.

"Perhaps you'd like to tell me about it," I pursued gently.

"I don't know much," the boy went on, looking up at me, his face flushed, his eyes wide and frightened, like those of a hunted stag. The three Granger boys adored their father; I had so often seen them going off with him on a Saturday afternoon to rugger matches, or on the tennis courts on summer evenings. I couldn't believe it.

"I know they quarrelled on Saturday because I heard them," Paul said blankly, his gaze back on the floor. "My room's just above theirs and Mum was crying; then when we got back from church yesterday morning Dad had gone."

He paused and bit his lip, fighting to hold back the tears.

"Mum told us last night that he wouldn't be coming back... There's another woman, someone he met through the office," he ended bitterly.

I didn't know what to say so I put my hand on Paul's clenched fist and pressed it, but he just kept looking hard at the floor.

Jacques came back into the dreary room.

"They're washing out her stomach," he said. "There's nothing we can do but wait."

And so we waited in silence, trying to encircle Paul with our love. I didn't think it worth stirring up more for the boy so I said nothing to my husband, but my stunned thoughts spun round and round asking the inevitable question. *Why*? And getting no reply.

I tried to pray, but no words came and this time it wasn't a silent worship and communion with God, but a blankness as if God were saying, "Where were you in all this?" And I couldn't understand what he meant. Then as the hours passed in that bleak waiting room, the monotony broken only by muffled noises and the shuffling of feet going backwards and forwards behind the closed swing door, Jesus came and sat beside me on that hard hospital bench and said:

"Look at me."

And when I looked into his eyes I saw a deep hurt.

"Where were you?" he asked.

And I had no answer, but this time I understood what he meant.

I had telephoned Anne the evening before, the day her husband had walked out on her for another woman, the day she was left to bring up five children alone, and I hadn't known. I was her friend and yet she hadn't felt she could turn to me for help or sympathy.

"Do you see what I mean?" Jesus said gently.

And I nodded.

"Do others see the difference in your life because of me?" Jesus went on.

And I knew they didn't.

If Anne had seen Christ in me, she would have known where to come, which door to knock on when tragedy struck, where to seek comfort and find someone to cry with. If Jesus' light had shone around me, if his love had been flowing through me and bubbling out like a fountain touching all those with whom I came into contact, as it should have been, then it would have been obvious to Anne.

I picked up Jacques' Bible which he had grabbed as we ran from the house and had now left lying on the bench when he went off seeking news for the second time. As I did so I glanced up at the clock on the wall. Both hands pointed to three and the hospital was very still. There was a marker inside the Bible, a drawing of Snoopy which Yves had done for his father's birthday and, as it automatically fell open at that place, words from Isaiah, which Jacques had underlined, stood out from the rest of the page.

"All your good works are like filthy rags in my sight."

I saw what God meant and I stood exposed before him for what I had almost become – a religious hypocrite.

Jacques came back and sat down beside Paul.

"They've taken your mother into the intensive care unit," he said quietly.

Paul looked up at him questioningly, his eyes full of fear.

"The doctors think she's going to be all right," Jacques continued reassuringly, "so we'll take you home now and I'll come back with you early in the morning."

He looked up at the clock and yawned. It was twenty minutes past five.

"Well," he smiled, "a little later than this; I'll pick you up about eight."

I realised that there were practical difficulties to be solved but Paul was adamant that he and Nickie could manage.

"Greet's been away for a long weekend," he said, "and should have got back on the last train. She always takes Alice to school on the way to her classes and Thérèse will be there before she leaves to look after Sophie. Really, there's no problem."

I'd forgotten about Anne's solid Dutch au pair and her wonderful "daily" and felt reassured that perhaps they could manage on their own for the time being. Anyway, five thirty in the morning wasn't the time to argue, so we dropped Paul off outside his darkened house to get a couple of hours' sleep.

Later that morning I went back to the hospital to see Anne. She lay still and lifeless on the narrow bed, her long dark hair framing a face pinched and drained of all colour. I was shocked to see how her once round, smiling features had become pointed, her cheek bones standing out in sharp relief below her sunken eyes.

The white-haired woman sharing the room looked over at Anne's bed and grimaced significantly as I walked past her.

"Doesn't look too good, does she?" she said grimly. "Hardly come round since they brought her in."

"She's had a bad time," I answered for want of something better to say.

The older woman turned back to her magazine and I sat down by Anne's bed and waited. Eventually, she opened her eyes. I hadn't noticed before how beautiful they were, green with hazel flecks, but that morning they were filmed over with sleep and her lids dropped slowly over them, her eyelashes lying like small black brushes on that ashen face.

"How good to see you," she murmured.

I bent closer; her words were soft and slurred and barely audible.

"Anne," I whispered, "why didn't you tell me?"

Her eyes remained closed and she did not answer immediately.

"You are so busy," she said softly and drifted off to sleep again.

I waited a little longer, but she didn't come round so, after half an hour, I tiptoed from the room. Her words had stung and humbled me, but they had confirmed what Jesus had put on my heart the night before.

As I walked slowly towards the exit, a tall figure came

bounding up the hospital stairs two at a time.

"Charles," I gasped, as we almost collided in the doorway.

Anne's husband stopped and looked at me unbelievingly. He was a handsome man, lean and athletic, his blond good looks a perfect foil for Anne's small, dark beauty, but that morning his face was drawn and haggard.

For a moment neither of us spoke.

"Anne?" he gasped.

"She's asleep," I answered.

"Yes, but..." He bit his lip and his blue eyes were frightened.

"She's going to be all right," I said quietly.

Charles looked down at the ground and pulled nervously at his moustache.

"I wasn't in the office when Paul rang," he said hesitantly. "I've only just got the message."

There was a pause; I suppose we were each waiting for the other to speak.

"I never thought she'd do that," he muttered, his voice hardly above a whisper. "I can't believe it."

I didn't reply immediately and we stood facing each other in an awkward silence.

"She must love you very much," I said at last.

He looked away, his face working, obviously moved and searching for a reply. Then suddenly I found the words spilling out.

"If you stray from the laws of God," I heard myself saying, "this is what happens."

He looked at me cautiously, as if seeking an answer.

How had I dared say that to him? They were Catholics, but even when Charles was home at the weekends he rarely went to church with his family. I knew it had not been me speaking. The Holy Spirit had put those words into my mouth, had helped me to see him as a child whom God loved and had prevented the sharp, unpleasant accusations which had risen in my throat when I bumped into him.

"But Jesus can change it all," I went on quietly. "He can bring good out of evil; he's just taught me that."

On my lips was a silent prayer for that little family, that Jesus would indeed make all things new.

Charles looked at me intently, swallowed hard, then

pressed my shoulder with his hand and turned towards the ward.

When I entered the house it was full of the afternoon stillness and I went straight upstairs and collapsed in the comfortable old rocking chair in which I had so often nursed the children. I felt spiritually as if I were back to square one, but the strain of the previous night and the shock of seeing Anne lying so pale and still on the hospital bed had cleared something in my brain. I confessed my failures and once again opened my heart to Jesus.

He gently lifted me up and showed me that what he wanted was *me*, that I was precious to him as I was, I didn't have to prove myself in any way. He revealed to me that he wanted fellowship with me as much as I needed fellowship with him, it wasn't a one-way communication, and the realisation was humbling; the Lord of all creation wanted me, just as I was.

And I saw that humility had been what was lacking in my new Christian life and that without it Jesus cannot work through us. That it is only when we are hiding behind his cross, clinging to it, claiming nothing for ourselves, that the power of God can pour itself into our lives and flow outwards like a fountain splashing over on to others. And I rose from my rocking chair humbled, but cleansed, knowing that Jesus had brought me painfully another step on my Christian walk.

Not because we think we can do anything of lasting value by ourselves. Our only power and success come from God. (2 Corinthians 3: 5) (The Living Bible)

11

THE PHONE CALL

The chintz curtains were drawn against the wind which had been sighing all day and had now sprung up in earnest; only one lamp was lit and the log fire's flickering flames playing against the old furniture and lighting up the rose pattern on the chair covers gave a feeling of warmth and security. I settled a cushion at my back and stretched my legs out on to a footstool, revelling in my material comforts.

Jacques stirred in the armchair opposite me and dropped his newspaper. He looked tired and drawn and I realised what a strain the previous night must have been.

"Have you any news of the Granger children?" he enquired. "I didn't say anything at dinner because the boys don't appear to know about what's happened, but now they're out of the way I think we should ring up and find out."

"I bumped into Charles as I was leaving the hospital," I said as I dialled the number. "He seemed stunned."

"Not surprising," remarked my husband drily.

Paul answered the call. It was his old voice, strong and crackling, without the fear of the previous evening.

"We're *fine*," he said in answer to my query. "There's no problem at all. Dad's here. Do you want to speak to him?"

I hesitated.

"Here he is," said Paul, before I could think further.

"Thank you *so* much for all you've done," Charles' voice came down the line.

I didn't know what to say.

"How's Anne?" I mumbled.

"Much better," he went on. "I've only just left the hospital. The drugs are wearing off but she's still very sleepy; it'll be a few days before she'll be well enough to come home."

He paused and I could hear his rapid breathing.

"I told her we'd go away together, just the two of us, as soon as she's strong enough."

He paused again.

"It must be years since we got off on our own without the children," he ended quietly.

There was an awkward silence.

"I know what you mean," I murmured. "It's not always easy."

"Nothing's easy," Charles replied slowly. "And it can't have been easy for Anne these past few months. I must have been out of my mind."

"The devil has a very subtle way of attacking," I said.

Charles gave a short, embarrassed laugh.

"That's one way of putting it," he answered.

And I could picture his face as I remembered him, relaxed and happy, without the terrible fear and tension I had seen on it that afternoon.

"I've promised Anne I'll take her to Greece," he went on. "She's always wanted to go and Easter will be the ideal time."

"Oh, how wonderful," I breathed.

But even as I said it, half of me did not really believe what I was hearing and we lapsed into a momentary silence. Yet I felt the conversation was not over, that Charles had more he wanted to say.

"Anne's always been rather cagey about leaving the children," he went on, "but I think I'll be able to convince her."

"I'm sure you will," I answered warmly, wondering what would happen when the holiday was over, whether once the emotional upheaval had settled down the other woman would creep in again.

"I told Anne this evening," Charles continued, "that if she'd like it I'll apply for a transfer. Paris has never really been her scene, she prefers a quieter life without all the tensions of a big city . . . and maybe we'd all be happier in a smaller place where I don't have to travel so much."

He paused uncertainly and I looked across at Jacques who was listening in on the other receiver. He nodded and smiled.

"Oh Charles," I breathed "we'd be sorry to lose you all but I'm sure if you both want it, that would be right."

"I think," he ended quietly, "we both do want it."

I replaced the receiver and sank gratefully back into my armchair.

"Father," I murmured, "thank you that out of evil you can bring good."

And I determined once again that from then onwards life would be different and I would recapture that close walk with Jesus which had been mine the summer before.

The lengthening days made life easier for me. Getting out of bed wasn't the problem it had been during the cold, dark winter mornings and I plunged back into my earlier routine of greeting the Lord before greeting my family and keeping that early morning hour sacred between Jesus and me, before the doorbell, the telephone, the children and their needs staked their claim. And gradually the deep peace and sense of purpose returned. I stopped rushing from meeting to meeting in an attempt to justify myself and prove my good Christianity; I "quietened down" and waited for the Lord to work through me and, as I did so, things began to change.

I didn't see Anne when she came out of hospital. She was only at home for a few days before they left for a family holiday in a house they rented every Easter in Britanny and, as soon as the children returned to school for the summer term, Charles took her off on the promised trip to Greece.

Paul and Nickie came round to the house as often as before but never mentioned that eventful night. As far as they were concerned, it was a chapter in their lives which they had completely wiped out of their minds, and although I was not entirely convinced that this was a good thing, I respected their silence.

"Have you heard the Grangers are moving?" Hervé enquired one afternoon as he walked in from school and flopped down on the grass beside me.

I looked up from my deck-chair enquiringly.

"No," I replied. "Must say I haven't seen anything of them for weeks. When did you hear?"

"Paul told me this morning," Hervé continued, leaning on one elbow, twiddling a daisy between his lips.

"Where are they going?" I enquired.

"You'll never believe it." Hervé paused, waiting for just the right effect. "To the *States*."

"The *States*," I echoed. "When?"

"Now," he said, triumphantly, looking around at the impact on his interested audience. The others had tumbled in after him and were sprawled around my deck-chair, listening intently. It wasn't often he had the floor. "At least, his Dad's starting his new job in July and they're moving over during the holidays."

I didn't say anything, and for a moment I felt a twinge of anger that Anne hadn't let me into the secret before.

As I picked up the receiver and Anne's voice came on the line I realised that the last time I had heard it was that day at the hospital when she had closed her eyes and murmured that I was so busy. And, for a split second, I felt embarrassed and didn't know what to say. But Anne didn't notice; she was bubbling.

"How *lovely* to hear you," she enthused. "I've been trying to get hold of you all day but I suppose now it's too late."

She broke off and laughed.

"Too *late*?" I echoed, puzzled.

"I wanted to tell you myself," she went on, "before the boys spread the news around. We only got back from New York last night and until then it wasn't definite, but now it's signed and settled I'm sure they've told all their friends. They were *so* excited."

She sounded excited too.

"Anne," I said, "let's meet."

"Yes let's," she replied warmly. "Just like old times."

"How about tomorrow?" I enquired.

"Lovely," she replied. "Come round for coffee and I'll tell you all about it."

Anne was busy pulling up weeds in the front garden when I arrived. She stood up, straightened her back and smiled. She had put on weight and looked radiant, the frightened eyes which had looked up at me from the hospital bed now bright and sparkling.

"I'm so happy to see you," she said, embracing me warmly. For a moment our eyes met and communicated and I knew that the page had turned and no further words were necessary. We walked into the house and sat down by the open window as she poured out the coffee.

"I can't believe it's happened," she murmured. 'It's like a

miracle, everything has fallen into place so wonderfully. Charles never dreamt he would be offered this job. It came out of the blue just before he asked for a transfer. I . . . have never been terribly happy in Paris."

"I know," I encouraged.

She looked down and bit her lip.

"I did try," she went on.

"That's the past," I said quietly.

She looked up at me and smiled, then leant back in her chair, completely at peace.

"This move has solved so many problems," she continued, gazing dreamily out of the window. "We've got a lovely house over there, with a stream at the bottom of the garden, and the girls will be able to have a pony."

She picked up the coffee-pot and refilled my cup.

"My mother came from Boston," she went on, "so, in a way, it's like going home."

She looked across at me, her eyes shining.

"Oh," she breathed, "God is so good."

I looked up in surprise. I had never heard her mention God before in that way and, remembering her words to me in the hospital, I felt hot with shame, realising that she had, no doubt, never heard me mention him either.

"Have you really met him Anne," I asked, "like I have, as your personal Saviour?"

She looked across at me and her lovely face was radiant.

"Yes," she breathed, "we both have, Charles and I."

"Charles?" I queried, utterly taken back.

Anne gave a slight laugh.

"I know it might seem impossible . . ."

"Not impossible," I was quick to add, "just rather surprising."

"Sometimes," Anne went on, "we have to be flat on our backs, down there in the depths of the pit, before we can see the stars. It's only then you look up and discover them. Otherwise when life is going well, we're always rushing around doing our own thing and never find the time to take our eyes off the ground."

I nodded. I knew what she meant.

"I met Jesus in that hospital," she said. "I'd been going to church all my life and thought I was a Christian . . ."

"So had I," I encouraged.

"But it wasn't until I was in the depths of despair that he became real to me. There was a nurse . . . the second night I was there, she sat by my bed and talked to me, opened my eyes to the truth and led me to know Jesus as my personal Saviour. My life has completely changed ever since."

"And Charles?" I enquired.

"I think when I came out of hospital he was so shattered that the soil was ready for sowing. We went away and whilst we were in Britanny he 'just happened' to meet someone . . . oh, it's ridiculous when one comes to think of it, we'd been going to that cottage for years, but it was this time that it 'just happened'. It was odd. The boys should have been going fishing with him but at the last minute friends rang and invited them to go to Mont St Michel for the day, so Charles went off by himself and who should he meet but this lovely Christian man and they started to talk. Charles accepted Christ before we came home and life has been totally different ever since."

She turned and looked at me.

"I've proved to myself the truth of Romans 8: 28," she said softly, "and I *know* that all things work together for good for those who love the Lord."

We neither of us spoke for a few minutes and I knew we were both quietly praising God for what he had done in our lives.

The Grangers had left by the time we returned from our holiday and at Christmas we received a card from them, happy and excited about their new life. Then silence. But the following year as I opened their greetings a photograph fell out of the envelope. It showed Anne, small and radiant, standing in front of their lovely Connecticut house with her family gathered round her. Charles, smiling broadly, was towering above her, an arm thrown protectively round her shoulders, the three boys were clustered behind and Alice and Sophie were standing holding hands in front.

But it was Anne who caught my attention, she was holding something in her arms. At first it looked like a bundle of washing but as I took a closer look I gasped. No, it couldn't be true, but there was no mistaking the downy blond hair, so like Sophie's had been, peeping out from under the lacy shawl. I opened up the card. Each member of the family had signed and added their personal greeting and at the bottom Anne had written, "Charlotte-Anne, born September 30th," and Charles had added in his neat, precise hand "our cup of happiness is overflowing." I looked down at the photograph and gazed mistily at the baby in Anne's arms.

As I turned away and glanced through the window at the overcast December day, I closed my eyes remembering how nearly that family had been torn apart by tragedy and thanked God for the wonderful way he had worked in their lives and carried out his promise to make all things work for good to those who love him. It seemed he had even fulfilled the prophesy given on the last page of the Old Testament and truly "opened the window of heaven and poured his blessings down upon them".

The old clock in the hall wheezed and prepared to strike the hour and as the last chime rang out in the silent house bringing me back to reality, I looked again at the photo in my hand. I felt a momentary twinge of envy thinking of the baby I would never hold in my arms and my old broodiness threatened to return. But I reminded myself that I had turned forty and, as it says in Ecclesiastes: "There is a time for everything, a time to sow, a time to reap," and I mentally added "and a time to be content with what you have and not always be yearning for something more."

Despite all this, overwhelming victory is ours through Christ who loved us enough to die for us.
(Romans 8: 37) (The Living Bible)

12

JOURNEYING TOGETHER

I don't think the children had believed me that afternoon in May 1967 when I told them I'd changed. But now, as the months passed and we began to knit together as a family as never before, even they noticed that life was different.

I'd like to pretend that the boys stopped fighting, but it wouldn't be true. But I discovered that I was able to stand on the touchline and watch their matches as an amused spectator rather than be there, het up and angry, in the midst of the fray. And in the end these battles to the death, which they fought regularly over the years, fizzled out more quickly and occasionally we even ended up laughing at ourselves; something which had never happened before. No, as the months passed I was definitely learning detachment and the lighter touch.

Because I was more open, more willing to listen and go along with their points of view, to admit that although I didn't always understand their attitudes I was willing to try, the children came more than half-way to meet me and the little things which had so irritated me before no longer did.

The Holy Spirit opened my eyes to the truth that we always see our own worst faults in others, and especially in our children, and he showed me that I was forever nagging Olivier about his impatience and unloving attitudes simply because, subconsciously, I was trying to cover up those very traits in my own character.

I had always been rather ambitious and wanted to "do my own thing" and although I was very happy to have a family, I had often felt frustrated and envied other women who seemed to be rushing out to exciting jobs, racing off to business meetings and having their days filled with glamorous appointments.

But as I went deeper and deeper into God's Word, Jesus showed me that being a housewife and mother was *not* the task of a second-class citizen but a highly prized and difficult career, and from then onwards I threw myself into making it just that for me. I made a tremendous effort to do the things which I knew pleased my family and which, in reality, cost me very little and, in the end, it ceased to be an effort. All that I did in love for them became a joy because I was doing it for Jesus and words from Matthew's Gospel often came into my head: "Whatsoever you do for one of these my little ones . . . you do for me."

The Book of Ephesians showed me where a wife stood in relationship to her husband. It didn't say go out and do your own thing no matter what happens to your family, fulfil yourself, find yourself, be the boss. No, it clearly told me that in a Christian household we are all parts of the same body and that if one part of a human body hurts, be it merely the little toe, the rest of the body is out of gear. And I tripped over the dog and broke my toe. Limping around for the next two weeks proved this truth to me!

I also learned that Jacques is the head of our body, our home, and that I am subject to him, but that he is subject to Christ; and Christ had not only said that I should obey my husband, but that my husband should love and cherish me as he did his own body. And what person willingly hurts his own body?

As I fell in line in this way, accepting my husband's authority and his decisions in the big issues, it gave me a wonderful new freedom, that freedom I had craved as a "liberated" woman and never achieved.

Looking back, I sometimes wonder what would have happened had the older children been brought up in a home controlled by the Holy Spirit from their childhood, a home where Jesus was Master and their parents truly committed to him. But God had already taught me that looking over my shoulder into the past at what might have been was a waste of precious time and that all I could now do was pick up the pieces and try not to make the same mistakes with the rest of the family.

And as Jacques and I put all our plans, all our problems, before Jesus, asking him to guide us, I discovered what a beautiful new dimension it gives to a marriage when both partners have their eyes on him. It was wonderful to have achieved this unity before the big problems started to arise.

Hervé was the first to rebel, though rebellion is hardly the word, he just "dropped out". Our smiling, untidy, easy-going boy whom Christopher resembled, as the French would say, "like two drops of water", suddenly began to scoff.

I think the same wheels may have been set in motion in his elder brother's mind, but Olivier was more conservative and, in the sixties, young people hadn't begun to oppose everything their parents stood for quite so openly.

The first time I had sensed that latent rebellion in the children I was a relatively new Christian and may have reacted more out of hurt pride than in love, but as one by one the children turned away to seek the truth for themselves I grieved for them, because I knew that once the weeds begin to show up in the soil of our hearts it is so much more difficult for the good seed to take root. Once again I had forgotten that God does not make mistakes and, one morning as I sought Jesus, my Bible open on my lap, he came and sat down beside me.

"Do you remember what my disciples were like before they were converted?" Jesus asked. "They were angry, jealous, boastful, self-seeking, proud – like the world, in fact. But I didn't join in their anger or give up on them. I didn't expect them to become 'instant' anything. No, I met them, as I met you, at the point of their deepest need, then led them on from there, at their pace, with the finished picture of what I wanted them to be always before me. But I did not expect to achieve the final result without pain, frustration and fatigue, though I knew there would also be joy and immense satisfaction on the way."

And to help me, he pointed to the half-finished sweater I was knitting, which was lying in a basket beside me. On the front of the pattern, I had a picture of what the finished object would look like, but I knew that when I changed needles after the first rib the jumper would be far from completed. The task had only just begun and there was still a lot of hard work, of personal effort, perhaps irritation, even pulling out and starting again, to do before I achieved the desired result. But, through it all, I had that final picture in my mind; I *knew* what I was working towards and had the assurance that with time and patience I would get there in the end.

And that was how it was with the children.

"God does not have any spiritual grandchildren," Jesus continued, "only children. And each one must come to him by himself. You can teach them about me, but only they can make the choice to accept me or not, to experience that spiritual rebirth and know me as their personal Saviour."

And I at last realised that although I had met Jesus and knew him to be the answer, I could not compel the children to accept this truth second-hand. I could only pray that my Lord would open their eyes: and I took comfort in the words from Proverbs 22, Verse 6: "Teach a child to choose the right path and when he is older he will remain upon it." It doesn't say that the growing child, the adolescent, even the grown man, won't try many wrong paths before he returns to the right one, but it does give the assurance that he will return to the right one in the end. And as I looked back over the years I had tried to make it without the Lord, I saw that Jesus had been there all the time, gently jogging my life along, keeping me afloat, preventing disasters and waiting patiently in the wings for me to realise my own helplessness – and admit it.

I have discovered that the best way Satan can attack parents is at their weakest point – through their children. We can bear attack upon ourselves. We can even stand fast under persecution, but our hearts break when we see our children suffer and that is where Satan forces us to our knees – in more ways than one! It was a truth that became plainer to me as the years went by and my longing for Jesus made me the devil's target.

It was now the early seventies. The two older boys were at university, Olivier studying law and Hervé economics, and both had stopped going to church or making any pretence about following our beliefs. In his second year Hervé, who had a flat in Paris near the university, came home one weekend and announced that he had decided to drop out; four years studying for a degree was too long and he wanted to do something else. But what?

The "something else" turned out to be a delivery man for a local supermarket!

And not long afterwards, he turned up at home with the
van on his way to deliver a load in Versailles, our
neighbouring town! We were in the middle of lunch, but
when his little brothers saw him walk in wearing his
regulation blue overalls, they leapt up from the table,
thrilled, and rushed out into the road to admire the van,
absolutely delirious with excitement when he offered to give
them a ride round the village.

They both made absolutely sure that everyone they knew
saw them that bright winter afternoon. Had it been raining it
might have been easier for me to take but, being a fine day
and Wednesday, a mid-week holiday for French schoolchildren, *everyone* seemed to be on the streets and the two of
them hung out of the window attracting the attention of
anyone who might not otherwise have noticed.

I didn't say anything, but I found it very hard to accept.
Hervé, the promising university student, a drop-out,
running around in a grocer's apron, heaving crates of bottles
in and out of a supermarket. We were well-known in the
village; our children were expected to do the "right thing".
And I couldn't even pretend it was a holiday job; February is
right bang in the middle of the university year.

"Oh God," I moaned, "why? *What* is going to become of
him? He can't spend his life this way."

Then Jesus put his hand under my chin, and turned my
face upwards until I looked him full in the eyes.

"Why not?" he said simply.

And I had no answer.

"I worked with my hands," he went on.

I nodded.

"Leave him to me," he ended, "and try to remember, love
and humility go together. There is no room for pride in my
children. In my Kingdom there are no rich or poor, only
brothers and sisters."

Jacques took Hervé's drop-out more philosophically than
I did. But my brooding did not last for long because only the
next week life again took one of those unexpected
somersaults and I was catapulted out of my cosy existence
into the reality of life and death and the emptiness of human
success and pride, the ephemerality of our earthly life. When
a crisis comes what we so often think of as "important" turns

out to be trivial and of no importance at all. And the simple truth that it is people who matter, not the image with which we like to cloak them, finally hit home. Once again I came crashing to the ground when a telephone call jolted me back to basics and showed me life in its right perspective.

My mother was dying.

Trust in the Lord with all your heart, and do not rely on your own insight. In all your ways acknowledge him, and he will make straight your paths.
(Proverbs 3: 5-6) (Revised Standard Version)

13

I'M COMING

I had been doing my big monthly "shop", a job I heartily disliked and always postponed till there was no way I could put it off any longer. That afternoon as I rumbled to a standstill before our front door, the car piled high with groceries, I found a telephone message marked "Urgent" waiting for me. My mother had had a heart attack and was very ill. Would I ring back immediately?

For a moment I was stunned ... and then afraid; it was so unexpected. My parents had always been there, wonderful rocks on whom we could rely. They had taken the children for holidays, welcomed us to the house for Christmas, coped with so many little things, been loving grandparents and, in my complacent fashion, I'd taken it for granted that it would always be so. Now, suddenly, I came face to face with their mortality, and I remembered that twilit summer evening in their garden some years earlier when, young in Christ, I had bludgeoned them instead of lovingly presenting my Jesus. Since then, although they came to church with us when visiting, we had all skirted round this controversial issue, and I was sure that my mother had only met the Lord through the pages of the Anglican prayer book and not with her heart.

Slowly, I picked up the receiver and dialled my old home in England. Ellen's voice answered me on the other end of the line and I was immediately reassured; she was one of the many people who over the years had adopted my parents and made their home her home. My mother had a wonderful gift of hospitality and, throughout our childhood and adolescence, there had always been people coming to the house for meals, for weekends, for days off or for holidays and Ellen had been one of them. Now, after a lifetime of service as a nursing sister in a London hospital, she had retired, but still came often to spend a long weekend or a holiday with my parents.

How grateful I was to hear her familiar voice.

"Ellen," I asked anxiously, "how is she?"

Ellen did not answer immediately.

"Not too well, I'm afraid," she said at last. "That's why I rang you, I thought it best."

"How's Daddy?" I enquired.

"Pretty shocked," she replied, "but he's bearing up."

There was a pause, but I didn't want to let her go, I needed to keep talking, to know more.

"But what happened?" I went on.

"It's not very clear." Ellen hesitated. "She collapsed on Monday morning."

I gasped.

"But today's *Thursday*," I protested.

"I know," she soothed. "We didn't want to worry you before, but this morning the doctor said that perhaps we should let you know."

There was a pause whilst her veiled understatement sank in and the line seemed to crackle with electricity.

"I came for the weekend," I heard Ellen's voice from across the Channel, interrupting my thoughts, "and I stayed on. I can stay on indefinitely . . . I know how difficult it is for you to come, you have the children . . ."

"I'll come over as soon as I can," I broke in.

And hung up.

As in all difficult situations, I mechanically dialled Jacques' office number.

"Don't worry," he said soothingly when I blurted out my fears. "You just go, we'll manage."

I thrust a few things into a bag and took Christopher with me; he was an easy child and for some reason had always been my mother's favourite, possibly because he had been named Robert after her father. I thought it might give her pleasure to see him, and it would certainly take my father's mind off the situation to have him around.

When I left, I had no idea how long I would be away and, when I walked into my mother's bedroom that evening, I marvelled that I had even arrived in time; she didn't recognise me, just lay motionless propped on her pillows, a shaded lamp by her bedside. My father and Ellen both looked exhausted. They were neither of them young, they loved my mother dearly and the strain of the past few days was beginning to show. I told them both to go to bed and get some sleep and let me take over and, although they protested, in the end they gratefully gave in, the responsibility momentarily out of their hands.

That night I sat by the shaded light watching the still figure on the bed and, as I had done once before at a crisis point in my life, I took my Bible and opened it at random.

I didn't know what was going to happen to my mother, I didn't know what was going to happen to any of us, but this time I knew who was in control. And as I sat there, not even looking at the open page on my lap, I felt completely at peace and had the impression that Jesus was bringing me round full circle and giving me the opportunity to show his agape love, to serve and minister to my mother who for so many years had ministered to me. My eyes dropped to the open page and Jesus' words to Jairus in Luke 8 sprang out at me: "Only believe and she will be made whole."

I slipped to my knees beside my mother's bed and thanked my Lord. I believed then that he had given me a glimpse into the future, showing me the miracle he was going to perform in this motionless body. At the time, I hadn't grasped that when Jesus spoke of healing he didn't always mean physical healing, often the least important; no, he very often went into the deeper meaning of healing and meant the healing of the spirit so that it could enter into communion with him. I thought that this promise meant that I would once again see my mother standing amongst the roses in her garden, there at the door waiting to welcome us, sitting by the drawing-room fire, her hands moving swiftly over something she was making. But it wasn't that that Jesus meant; again he was leading me gently into his mysteries.

It had been a long, tiring day and I dozed off in the early hours of the morning into a fitful sleep and when I awoke there was a silver light creeping round the edge of the curtains. I rose and, drawing them aside, stood looking out on the still garden and over the flat expanse of the Essex marshes. A damp, heavy mist was curling on the horizon and the first streaks of dawn creeping up the lawn pinpointed tiny crocuses peeping out of the flowerbeds.

My mother stirred on the bed and opened her eyes. The curtain dropped from my hand and I went over to where she was lying. Her lips were moving and I bent close to hear what she was saying.

"What are you doing here?" she whispered.

I sat down beside her and smoothed her brow, not answering. I didn't know what to say.

"Go home to your children," she whispered.

And she smiled. It seemed as if life had begun to flow back into her.

There were movements downstairs and I heard the clatter of plates. Ellen came into the room with a cup of tea for me.

"Breakfast's ready," she whispered. "Then go and get some sleep. I feel wonderful after that long night."

My mother's eyes had closed again. Ellen looked down at her and turned to me enquiringly.

"She's had a good night too," I smiled, as I sipped the hot tea, "and she seems better. I don't feel like breakfast, I think I'll just go straight to bed."

Ellen nodded and took my mother's wrist in her capable fingers.

I crossed the landing and went wearily into my old room; the room I had had as a teenager, the room with my books and the pretty chintz curtains and windows looking out on to the garden, the room I had always been happy to come back to and, as always, the years dropped away and I felt young again, unburdened, without responsibilities. It had always been like that. Here in this room, I was no longer a middle-aged mum, but somebody's child again.

As I climbed gratefully into bed I could hear the murmur of my father's and Christopher's voices as they chatted together over breakfast in the dining-room below and it was a warm, comfortable buzz which lulled me to sleep.

The watery February sun was low in the sky when I awoke and lay watching the shadows play on the wall. There was a knock on the bedroom door and Ellen came in with the inevitable cup of tea.

"You must be starving," she said. "You haven't eaten a thing since yesterday evening."

"How is she?" I asked, not answering her question.

"Much the same," Ellen replied as she sat down on the side of the bed and watched me drink my tea.

"Wasn't it a blessing that I happened to have come for the weekend?" she went on. "I was leaving on Monday morning when it happened."

I nodded, knowing that nothing in God's plan for our lives happens by accident.

"Has it messed up your plans?" I queried.

"Not at all," she went on. "I can stay as long as I'm needed."

Ellen rose and went across the hall and into the sick-room. I didn't get up immediately but lay thinking, going back down the years. I knew that my mother had never had that personal encounter with Jesus which I had had, that total surrender and rebirth which I had experienced, and Jesus said:

"That is why you are here. I have spared her so that she may know me."

Ellen's head appeared round the door.

"Geoffrey will be here in time for dinner," she said. "Thought you'd like to know."

And she disappeared down the stairs.

My brother and his family were stationed at that time in Canada and, after the message the Lord had given me the night before, I felt it was an unnecessary journey; it still had not irrevocably seeped into my understanding that the Lord does not make mistakes.

By the time I went downstairs, my brother had arrived and insisted on staying up that night. I sat in the darkened sick-room with him for a while and we talked softly together about the old days until I went off to bed for a few hours before relieving him in the early morning.

But he was suffering from jet-lag and was up again by midday. My mother didn't seem to be any better or any worse but, as everyone went into the drawing-room for coffee after lunch, I decided to go up and sit with her for a while.

Her eyes were open as I went into the room. I sat down beside the bed and took hold of her hands. She looked up at me and smiled as we remained there, her hand resting limply in mine, my free hand gently caressing her brow. It seemed natural and I remembered how, when I had had chickenpox at seven years old, she had done the same for me.

Suddenly, she tried to withdraw her hand from mine and her grey eyes looked up at me imploringly.

"Don't hold me back," she whispered, "they are all there, waiting for me."

My grip tightened on her hand and, for a split second, I was afraid. Then I relaxed, remembering the verse Jesus had given me on the night I arrived.

"Let me go," she pleaded, trying to raise herself from the pillows.

"I'll let you go," I answered softly, "when you get there. Just let me stay with you till you reach them."

She relaxed and let her hand rest in mine, a sweet smile on her lips, and I knew that this was the chance Jesus was giving me, perhaps the last chance, to lead her to him.

"Do you love Jesus?" I asked gently.

She didn't look at me, but motioned "yes" with her head. I leant forward.

"Tell him," I implored, "tell him. Just say, 'Jesus I love you.'"

Her lips moved and I heard the words come softly.

"Jesus I love you, Jesus I love you." And a third time, "Jesus I love you."

She lay back, completely at peace, then suddenly she raised herself on her pillows till she was sitting upright in the bed and stretched out her arms. Her face was radiant, like that of a young bride as she walks down the aisle and sees the man she loves waiting for her at the altar.

"Jesus," she said audibly, "Jesus, I'm coming... take me..."

Her arms dropped and she fell back on to her pillows with a deep sigh.

From the drawing-room beneath I heard the tinkling of coffee cups and a burst of laughter. I picked up her limp hand; her breathing appeared to have ceased and, as I looked at my mother lying serene and still on the bed, I wondered whether to call my father. Suddenly she took a deep breath and the motion of breathing started up again, slowly, painfully, and continued in this way throughout the day, though my mother did not regain consciousness.

She died three weeks later, but for me she died on that winter afternoon when her radiant face showed me that she had met Jesus and I understood then that when the Lord had told me, through his Word, not to fear, she would be made whole, he was not thinking of making her tired heart beat strongly again, but of making her spiritually whole, her eyes cleansed so that she would see him.

And as I stood under a tree in the old churchyard on that grey, windy, sleeting March day when, within sight of our house, her earthly remains were lowered into the ground, although my heart was heavy because I would not see her again on this earth and I hurt for my father who was now alone, I knew that that box about to be covered by sodden earth only contained the tired, earthly body my mother no longer needed, or wanted. That she was with Jesus and he would give her the new body he had promised, that body which would never grow old and die. And that, one day, we would meet again.

And I heard a loud voice from the throne saying, "Now, the dwelling of God is with men, and he will live with them. They will be his people, and God himself will be with them and be their God. He will wipe every tear from their eyes. There will be no more death or mourning or crying or pain, for the old order of things has passed away."
(Revelation 21: 2–4) (New International Version)

14

THE SCOFFER

I cried for my mother, or rather for myself, because I had loved her and I knew that the next time I went to my old home she would not be there. But, through this parting, I grew nearer to Jacques because I now understood what had astonished me so much when his mother died: that death need only separate us physically from our loved ones and that if we are in Christ and believe in the resurrection we know they are not lost to us forever.

Jacques and I also began to be aware of our own mortality as, Jacques' father having died the autumn before, my father was now the only grandparent left. And it was a shock to realise that we were creeping nearer the stage when we would be "the older generation" with no longer an earthly parent to lean back on and that one day I, like Jacques, would cease to be someone's child – in the human meaning of the word.

Although I didn't feel my mother's presence in the way Jacques had done, I was not as unhappy as I had expected to be because always there was that wonderful, comforting thought that I knew without any doubt that Jesus had come to take her and that she was with him. But she made her presence felt in another way.

That summer we were staying with my brother and his family in St Raphael in the South of France where my sister-in-law's family had a holiday house, when Christopher suddenly fell ill. He was a sturdy little boy of eight but for three days he lay in bed with a raging temperature which the doctors did not seem to be able to master. One afternoon, it must have been on the third day, everyone else had gone to the beach and I was sitting by his bedside in that quiet, shuttered room, holding his hot, limp hand as I had done a few months earlier for my mother.

Christopher's eyes were closed and there were beads of sweat on his forehead. My plump, rosy-faced little boy was now drained of colour and the dark shadows under his eyes pinpointed the contours of his cheeks which had lost their roundness even in those few feverish days.

Distracted and worried, I lifted his head and tried to get him to drink and as I gently laid him back on the damp pillow and wiped the perspiration from his forehead there in the stillness of that hot Mediterranean afternoon I heard my name called. It was so clear I looked round. But there was no one there; the house was empty and silent, no footsteps anywhere. I bent to fan his hot face and again I heard my name. It was my mother's voice, clear and unmistakable, and I suddenly felt the wonderful comfort and peace a lost child feels when she finds her mother in the crowd and rushes towards her knowing that the agony is over and everything will be all right.

There was no other sound, no other voice, but I had the feeling that in calling my name my mother was saying to me, "I am watching over him," and I relaxed, soothed and comforted.

I hadn't been thinking of my mother, in fact, I hadn't thought about her a great deal since she died, I had been so at peace about her end, but this call was so clear. And that night Christopher's temperature began slowly to drop.

I am sure the sceptics will find a rational explanation, and I am sure there are many. But for me it was as though I was able, from that moment on, to have peace knowing that my mother was with Jesus and that he had my child safely in his arms.

A few days later, Hervé arrived with some friends on their way to holiday in Corsica. We had vaguely expected him but what we didn't expect was the news he came to bring us. His career as a delivery man was over and he had decided to go back to university in the autumn, to start again, but not in Paris; this time he had registered in Montpellier. He had wasted a year, but had he really wasted it? I am sure he had benefited a great deal from those six months working long hours with his hands and learning some of the truth of what life is all about. Up till then Hervé's life had been the sheltered life of home, school and university, but those months on the road, rubbing shoulders with all kinds of people and finding out how they lived, had certainly not been wasted and, as I look back, was all part of God's plan for his life. I didn't see the complete picture then, but in Herve's case, too, God had not made a mistake!

The house was gradually emptying. Yves had gone to prep school in England the year before, my liberally-minded husband feeling that it would be good for the boys to have a taste of education on both sides of the Channel, since they were wholly French by nationality only – and Christopher was to follow his brother after Christmas. Olivier had obtained his law degree and was leaving to spend two years in Beirut in September and Bee was off to a school in the south of England to do a riding instructor's course.

From having too much to do, I now began to wonder how I was going to fill my days and clung desperately to Christopher as the last chick in the nest, dreading the time when I would stand on the platform at the Gare du Nord and wave him goodbye too. There were four other boys from our vicinity all at the same school in Kent, so the actual departure tended to be a hilarious affair, mercifully, as I was never able to bear actually taking my sons and leaving them at the school door. The boys themselves were blissfully happy, but I still hadn't quite grasped the full meaning of agape love and the fact that one has children for *themselves*, not for *oneself*, and the mother hen in me clucked and brooded.

But that summer was beautiful, almost like a last reunion. My father came to join us in St Raphael and seemed to be perfectly content, just watching his grandchildren, and as his eightieth birthday was on September 1st they all went to tremendous lengths to make it a memorable one. One boy painted a picture of the old Provençal farmhouse; Sarah and Fanny, my brother's little girls, made peculiar things out of raffia; Christopher, Yves and my nephew Pascal, who were all born within three years and so formed a "terrible trio", painted a banner with "Happy Birthday Grandad" in large letters. They then draped it on to the boat which was festooned with streamers and all climbed in, man-handling an enormous birthday cake. At the appointed signal, my brother having hooked the boat to the car, they all climbed in and he drove them past the terrace where the birthday hero had been installed, with all the grandchildren hanging over the side of the boat, waving streamers and yelling their heads off.

I don't know who enjoyed themselves most, my father, my brother or the children! It was a wonderful display of love and affection and it would have been a splendid occasion except that Pascal, in his excitement, leapt out of the boat, slipped and hit a stone, opening his leg rather badly, so had to spend the rest of the evening waiting to be sewn up in the local hospital, which rather dampened the festivities. But the memory was there and it was a grand finale to the last time we, as a family, were all together before they broke up and, like birds leaving the nest, began to fly in their different directions.

Hervé was due to leave for Montpellier at the beginning of October and, one Friday evening towards the end of September, Jacques and I decided to go into Paris to hear Donald Wilkerson, David Wilkerson's brother, who was speaking at a meeting. Knowing Hervé's feelings, I was pretty sure of his answer before I put the question, but something prompted me to ask him if he'd like to come with us all the same. The rebellious stage had passed and now, at twenty-one, he was just mildly amused that we should still believe in "that old fairy tale".

He looked up from his armchair by the crackling log fire and yawned.

"You'll never give up, will you?" he smiled. "No, you two run along and enjoy yourselves. 'Fraid your God-squad stuff isn't my cup of tea at all."

And getting up he walked with us to the door, waving gaily as our car started off up the hill.

I thought about Hervé all through the meeting, knowing that the gripping story of a young preacher who, armed only with his Bible, had gone into New York's underworld and succeeded in converting many of the toughest young thugs and their leader, would have appealed to him. As we left, there were books for sale and, although I had already read *The Cross and the Switchblade*, for some reason I bought a copy.

Hervé left for Montpellier a few days later, his old car

piled high with pots, pans and dishes stuffed in amongst his rugger kit and an arsenal of books and, as I went back into the house to get the thermos he had forgotten, I noticed *The Cross and the Switchblade* lying on the hall table.

It didn't look like a "religious" book. The jacket was colourful, showing a swarthy thug holding a knife to the chest of a startled young man; it could have been a modern thriller, just, in fact, the sort of book I'd so often seen Hervé relaxing with.

For a moment I hesitated then, picking it up, ran down the steps to the car. The engine was already humming as I pushed the book through the open window saying, as casually as my thumping heart would let me:

"I bought this the other day and thought you might like to read it; it's not long, but it's very exciting."

Hervé glanced at the cover and stuffed the book into the already overflowing glove compartment before setting the angry splutterings coming from the bonnet into a terrible roar as his car prepared to attack the nine hundred kilometres which would now separate him from us.

Jacques threw his arm round my shoulders as we turned to go back into the house.

"I'm glad you managed to give Hervé that book," he said. "I've been looking for an opportunity all weekend."

"I'd forgotten all about it," I replied, "knowing how 'anti' he is. But there it was, staring up at me when I went back into the house for his thermos. It seemed as if it were meant to be."

Jacques squeezed my shoulder.

"Well, let's see what happens," he said. "You never know, he might even read it."

We both laughed and went back into the now silent house.

Christopher was at the village school, Bee and Yves had left for England and Olivier was already in Lebanon and now the large, old house which had once rung incessantly with noise took on a different character.

Ever since we had become Christians, we had both prayed for each one of the children every day and very especially as they grew up and began to seek for the truth themselves. Now, as I went round the house clearing up after Hervé's departure, I earnestly prayed that he would find joy and satisfaction in this new life. Up till then, home had always been round the corner when he needed it, but now like Olivier and Bee he was alone, in a strange town, new friends to make, new studies to conquer. He was very much in my thoughts during those crisp autumn days.

But as one door closes, in the Lord's perfect plan, another always opens; and Jean-Louis came into our lives. The children had been the first to notice him; he always seemed to be hanging out of a window in the chateau next to our house which had been sold and turned into a centre for further education. And it wasn't long before they began to talk to him and then invite him home. Jean-Louis was thin and wiry with quick nervous gestures: his sallow complexion and his fine dark hair receding from his temples gave him the inscrutable look of a red Indian chieftain. He was a shy, taciturn man, sometimes abrupt and confusing in his attitudes but, as he came to know us and realised that we accepted him as he was, he opened up and warmed to us and became part of the family. So much so that I ceased to bother when he was in the house, merely greeting him if I found him around or automatically setting another place if he turned up at meal-times.

Little by little, we learned his story and it was not a happy one. He was completely without family, never having known his father and having been abandoned by his mother to foster parents at an early age. Now, at thirty-eight, after trying all kinds of jobs and religions all over the world, he was working in the archives of the chateau and living alone in the room they had provided. He appeared to have no friends and pretended he didn't need any, but as we got to know him and slowly uncovered the layers of masks he had built round himself, we discovered a sensitivity and sweetness which would occasionally trickle through, only to be abruptly quenched when he felt himself becoming involved. So we just took him as he was and he began to be a regular feature at our birthday and Christmas celebrations, where his dammed-up love would come pouring out as he arrived with expensive presents, each one carefully chosen and wrapped for the person concerned. The children had a very happy relationship with him and, despite the age gap, I would often find him with one or the other of them, chatting in their rooms.

Now that the nest was almost empty, Jean-Louis called more frequently and, although neither of us mentioned it, I think he knew in a way that perhaps Jacques didn't understand, the emptiness I felt after years of having my brood around me, busy caring for them, loving them, worrying about them and often being driven frantic by them, but at least I was needed and had a purpose in life. I had been fulfilled and satisfied to the hilt. Now a new era was opening before me and I wasn't sure I was going to like it very much.

Jean-Louis in his own deprivation and loneliness seemed to sense that and I would sometimes find those strange dark brown eyes of his watching me, almost as a mother watches a toddler, arms outstretched to catch him if he falls. There was an unspoken bond between us and I began to see what the boys saw in him, a sweetness and a sensitivity, sometimes almost a naïveté.

I kept busy and watched the postman but none of the children were famous for their writing skills. The school set time for Yves to write every Sunday and his spelling mistakes and peculiar turns of phrase formed an amusing part of my week. Olivier was perhaps the most dutiful; he had always been a boy of discipline and it had gone on into manhood, but troubles were starting up in Beirut and the post was erratic. Bee was in love at the time and although she did write, most of the news came to us via the boy friend she had left behind. Hervé blamed the fact that he had been dyslexic as a child for his lack of postal communication. I put it down to laziness, but that was another thing!

It was one morning in mid-December, when I was in the full flurry of Christmas preparations, that the letter arrived. I sat down eagerly to read it. News from Hervé was so rare and, as my eyes quickly scanned the pages, tears began to blur the closely written sheets and stream uncontrollably down my cheeks. As I came to the end, I heard the telephone ringing in the hall below.

Yves was home on holiday and busy gluing paper garlands together to decorate the dining-room.

"Mum," he shouted up the stairs. "Dad calling from the office."

I went into our bedroom and picked up the receiver, my voice choked with emotion.

"Whatever's the matter?" came Jacques' anxious voice down the line.

I took a deep breath.

"We've just had a letter from Hervé," I answered, and began to read.

"This is an advance Christmas present," he had written two days earlier, "probably the most beautiful present you will ever receive from me and one I know you've always longed to have."

"Yes," said Jacques impatiently, "go on, what's happened?"

But the letter was long and I wasn't sure I could stem my tears indefinitely, so I put it down and simply told my husband what had happened to our scoffer son.

As I had hoped, he had taken the book I tossed into his car for a thriller and, one evening, alone in his new surroundings, had picked it up and begun to read. The story had gripped him. The following week there had been a Christian rally in the lively university town and, although he hadn't intended to go, Hervé said that on the first evening he felt as if he were being propelled in that direction.

The meeting had gripped him, too, and he had returned to the tent each evening and on the Saturday, when the rally ended, our son had been one of the many whose lives had been changed. As he explained in his letter:

"I didn't write to tell you as soon as I was converted because the experience was too deep and I wanted to have time to test my emotions." But he went on: "I now believe that Jesus is the way, the truth and the life and that he died for me and I have asked him to come into my life and be my personal Saviour."

For a moment neither of us spoke then, obviously deeply moved, Jacques said quietly:

"I'll be home early."

And rang off.

That evening, for us as a couple, was one of wonderful communion with Jesus. God had promised us in his Word that if we brought the children up to follow the right path, when they were older they would not depart from it, and here we had that first proof before us. He had been so gracious, and we felt so unworthy. Hervé had come back, Olivier and Bee were still out of the realm of his love, but this wonderful assurance of the promise he had given us filled us with hope and joy that one day he would bring them both back into his fold if only we would trust and have patience.

I went to bed glowing in the warmth of God's love, sure that this Christmas, when all the children would be home, would be a very special celebration and I looked forward confidently for more miracles in our daily walk with him.

Thou wilt show me the path of life: in thy presence is fulness of joy.
(Psalm 16: 11) (King James' Version)

15

"PRAY IF YOU LIKE"

It was the final countdown, only days to go before Christmas and excitement at its height. The two youngest could hardly contain themselves and, as it was Wednesday and the usual school half-holiday for Christopher, I had sent him off with Yves to the park with the dogs to get rid of their energy and leave me alone to finish some last-minute jobs.

Suddenly, the December afternoon was broken by the sound of a slow, heavy step coming into the house. I looked up from my wrapping paper wondering who it was. It wouldn't be the boys, they always sounded like a landslide and anyway the dogs never entered the house unheralded. I went into the hall and there in a corner crouched Jean-Louis.

"Why, Jean-Louis," I cried, "whatever's the matter?"

For a moment he remained silent, just stared at me with those dark impenetrable eyes then, as if coming out of a stupor, replied:

"I've just been to the hospital."

I hardly dare enquire if anything was wrong. He dragged himself slowly into the room and slumped on to the window seat, staring miserably in front of him. Then, after an agony of waiting, "I've got cancer," he blurted out. "They said six months, a year at the most."

The full impact of what he had said took a few minutes to sink in. I knew he had not been feeling well and had lost weight but – between that and six months to live!

I went over and took his arm.

"Come and sit by the fire," I said gently.

He didn't seem to hear, just crumpled into the armchair I led him to.

"Are you *sure* it's true?" I asked.

"That's what the specialist said," he replied without looking up.

"And have they done all the tests?" I insisted. "Is it absolutely definite?"

Jean-Louis nodded slowly, his eyes staring fixedly into the flames, and I didn't know what to say.

I felt a sudden overwhelming surge of anger at the unfairness of life. His had been such a sad one. But, at the same time, Jesus' words to his disciples in John 16, "the Father will give you whatever you ask him for in my name", rang in my head.

"Jean-Louis," I said gently, after we had sat like this for some time, with only the sound of a log dropping deeper into the ashes to disturb the heavy stillness of the room, "I know you don't believe in anything and the future seems hopeless to you now, but... would you let me pray with you about this?"

He didn't reply, just remained staring blankly into the glowing fire. I didn't insist but sat quietly with him in the eerie twilight, my heart aching to comfort him.

The hall clock struck five and the short winter afternoon was almost over. The boys would be rushing in soon out of the gathering darkness, maybe they would help relieve this dreadful tension. Then, as if drawing his thoughts laboriously back from a dreadful abyss, Jean-Louis said flatly:

"Pray if you like."

I reached over and took his hand in both of mine; he didn't resist but there was no answering touch, it was as if all life had been extinguished in that crumpled body. We sat there like that, and no words came.

"Oh Father," I whispered brokenly at last, "Jean-Louis is your child, you created him and you love him and now I hold him up to you and ask you to put your healing touch on his sick body and make him whole."

Jean-Louis didn't move. He gave no sign of even having heard, and when I gently released his hand it dropped to his side like a dead weight.

In the distance I heard the clatter of feet as the boys raced across the courtyard.

"Oh, hi, Lulu," they said as they burst into the room and ran to warm their hands in front of the glowing fire. "Why aren't you at the office?"

I got up and put my hand on his shoulder.

"We'll have an early dinner," I said in a matter-of-fact tone. "You stay and have it with us."

And I went into the kitchen. The boys' direct approach seemed to jerk him out of his misery for when I peeped in on my way to set the table the three of them were hunched over the Scrabble board. It was Jean-Louis' favourite game, and he always won. Had the boys an intuition I lacked?

The next day the house was filled with noise and laughter as one by one they all arrived home and in the excitement of being together, we forgot: Jean-Louis was around, but we were used to his silence and didn't take much notice. And so Christmas came and went, and in the days immediately following, Jean-Louis was in and out as much as ever; he had stopped smoking and looked grey, but he seemed to have accepted his illness and come to terms with it. He never mentioned it again and if we broached the subject he became prickly, but Jacques and I continued to pray that God would heal him.

The day after New Year he suddenly appeared in the kitchen just before lunch, looking ashen and more haggard than ever; his dark, haunted eyes seemed completely to fill his sallow face.

"I'm going to Paris," he announced abruptly. "The hospital rang; the specialist wants to see me immediately."

I looked at him without saying anything and knew that he feared bad news, that the disease had escalated more quickly than anticipated and he had not even the promised six months to live.

"I'll come with you," I said, quickly untying my apron. "The family can get their own lunch."

But he brushed me aside.

"No," he replied roughly, "I'm catching the next train – in ten minutes."

"Well, come straight back here and let me know what's happened," I called, running down the steps after him.

"*If* I come back," he threw grimly over his shoulder. "I've packed a bag... in case."

He looked at me almost accusingly and then he was gone. I knew what he was thinking, "you and your prayers", and, miserably, I went back into the house.

"Oh God," I cried as I stirred the gravy, "how can I make

Jean-Louis see that no matter what happens, whatever he feels, you love him? He has so little and I have so much."

He'd never put it into words, but I had often felt an unspoken: "It's all right for *you*," in his strange dark eyes.

The short winter day dragged slowly on. Snow had fallen in the night and the children had all gone off into the park with the sledge, leaving the house unbearably empty and silent after the excitement of the last few days. I didn't want to go out in case Jean-Louis should come back and every chime of the clock in the silent emptiness seemed to sound a death knell in my troubled thoughts. There was so much to do to clear up the post-Christmas disorder, yet I couldn't settle to anything.

At four o'clock, in an effort to take my mind off brooding, I made a cup of tea and took the newspaper to read by the fire and it was as I was closing the drawing-room curtains against the gathering dusk that I saw Jean-Louis walking across the garden.

"Oh Father," I whispered, "give me the words, tell me what to say to him."

And then even my prayer seemed to stick in my throat. I heard him enter the house and still I didn't move but, suddenly, I knew he was in the room and slowly I turned round.

"Come and sit by the fire," I chanted, as if reciting lines from a play, and I realised the absurdity of the situation. This was how it had all begun. I managed to smile and he smiled back.

"They didn't want to keep you in hospital then?" I heard myself saying.

"No," answered Jean-Louis, and he smiled again.

His smiles were rare, but very beautiful, like a sudden radiance lighting up his whole face.

"In fact," he continued, "they don't want to see me any more."

This time no words came from me.

"I saw the Big White Chief," Jean-Louis continued quietly. "They were all very embarrassed; it seems there's been a mistake."

"A mistake?" I echoed foolishly, gripping the arms of my chair tightly.

"Yes – a terrible mistake."

He turned to face me, his back to the crackling logs, and the radiance suddenly disappeared from his face.

"A terrible mistake," he said again, "for another Jean-Louis Duval, who spent a happy Christmas thinking he only had bronchitis."

"I don't understand," I gasped.

"It's quite simple," he went on. "In these big hospitals case histories occasionally get muddled, not often, but it does happen and it happened this time. Duval's a pretty common name," he continued, sitting down in the armchair opposite me, "and it just happened that two Jean-Louis Duvals went for a consultation about the same time with the same symptoms. One had cancer and one didn't."

He looked across at me, his face taut, but the dark shadows had gone from under his eyes.

"I'm the one who didn't," he ended quietly.

"Oh Jean-Louis," I cried out, "you mean..."

"I mean that I had a bad attack of bronchitis last winter which never really went away and I've got to have a course of injections to clear up the remains. It's the other chap who's now got to be told he has no future."

"Jean-Louis," I whispered, "I'm so glad."

"So am I," he replied, "... in a way."

I looked at him aghast.

"What do you mean," I burst out, "in a way?"

He didn't reply immediately. Then, looking across at me intently, he said quietly:

"Just that having lived with a death sentence for over two weeks, I know exactly how the other Jean-Louis Duval's going to feel when they break the news to him – if they haven't already done so."

For a moment neither of us spoke. I saw what he meant. Then Jean-Louis said simply:

"Perhaps you'd better ask your God for a miracle for him too."

Once again I could think of nothing to say. I understood his feelings; his rejoicing was overshadowed by the anguish of knowing what another man, bearing his name, would have to suffer and come to terms with. I bowed my head.

"Lord Jesus," I said. "You who are the great healer, you who love us and know every hair on our heads, you who came into the world to save sinners and heal the broken-hearted, we hold this man up to you now, this other Jean-Louis, and we ask you to put your healing hands on him. We don't know anything about him, we don't know whether he is alone, if he has a family, if he has little children depending on him and, most important, we don't know if he loves you. But you know all these things, Father, and so we leave him in your hands claiming your promise in Romans 8 to make 'all things work for good for those who love you'. May some good come out of man's terrible mistake ... and thank you, Father."

There was a pause and then to my great surprise I heard Jean-Louis quietly say:

"Amen."

I thought then of the wonderful events of the past month, Hervé's letter, Jean-Louis' escape from death and I looked forward to the year which had just begun with hope in my heart. Mercifully, God turns the page for us day by day, gives us courage just for that fleeting moment and tells us not to worry about tomorrow. Mercifully, he did not open the book of life and give me a glimpse of the morrow, or my joy would have been extinguished. Little did I know that I was approaching my testing time, the time when I would learn what it really was to be alone with only God to cling to, when all that would be left of my world – my cosy, sheltered, secure, loving world which I had built around me – would be ... hope.

This is the assurance we have in approaching God: that if we ask anything according to his will, he hears us.
(I John 5: 14) (New International Version)

16

EARLY ONE MORNING

The high pitch of excitement over, Olivier went back to Beirut, Hervé to Montpellier, the three others to England and, with Christopher now gone, the house echoed once more with the silence and I had not yet found anything constructive to do.

On the outside, I was still the same loving wife, the strong Christian friend, the counsellor, upholder of the faith, but on the inside there were rumblings of anger and discontent. I was forty-eight and had reached the end of my maternity. I knew it but didn't want to accept it, to accept that that phase of my life had ended and that another one was about to begin. I was running towards my destination, and inside I rebelled and looked for someone to blame. And, as always, Jacques was there. Instead of turning to Jesus and asking him to help me, I turned on my husband and accused him of having sent my children away.

I knew it was stupid, I knew it was untrue, I knew it was a decision we had taken together, but I wanted a scapegoat. A certain coolness sprang up between us. Not on his side – he was as loving and kind as ever – but on mine: with the children gone, I refused to listen to reason of any kind and decided that life was finished.

That may explain why not much more than a week after the house emptied I wasn't terribly concerned when Jacques came home one evening and said he wasn't feeling very well.

"I'm feeling pretty whacked, I think I'll have an early night," he said over his shoulder as he headed for the stairs. "Sorry about dinner, perhaps you can keep it until tomorrow."

I don't think I even noticed his ashen face, just shrugged in annoyance, turned off the stove and, picking up my book, flopped down by the drawing-room fire.

He left next morning before I was awake. I didn't realise that at last it was my husband's turn to have some of the attention he had been denied during the children's growing years. I just assumed he could manage as he had always done: and up till then he did. But a couple of hours later, when I was looking out of the window waiting for the postman and watching a grey January drizzle crawl down the window-panes, the telephone rang.

It was my husband's secretary. Jacques had had a heart attack at the office and was now on his way to a large Paris hospital.

It had been an action-packed year. The successive series of crises had hit us back and forth like ping pong balls, but now it was action-stations again as the shock of coming face to face with my husband's mortality hit me full on. And I realised that I had been wallowing in self-pity ever since the day I had waved Christopher goodbye and finally come home to an empty house.

As I raced to the hospital not knowing what to expect, I realised that the house had been far from empty: Jacques had been there with me and, as fear and remorse mingled with my prayers, I cried out for the chance to be alone with him again in that house which we had so lovingly made into our home.

Jacques had been taken to the intensive care unit and the smiling faces of the nurses and their calm manner reassured me.

When I was shown into his room he looked up and smiled.

"Don't worry," he said gently, taking my hand as I sat down on the chair beside his bed.

"What happened?" I asked.

"Oh, just a scare," he answered reassuringly. "I don't know why they're making so much fuss."

"Must be a reason," I mumbled.

Jacques patted my hand.

"Perhaps they're short of patients," he joked.

I looked down at him, trying to understand. He appeared tired, but otherwise the same as usual and I felt momentarily reassured. We sat in silence for a little while and I remember thinking defensively, "it wasn't like this when I was in training" as I heard the raised voices of the nurses in the corridor outside his room.

"They could shut up," I muttered, to break the silence.

"Not like when you were nursing?" Jacques teased.

And I took the bait.

"No," I snapped angrily.

"Don't worry," he soothed. "In spite of the noise, they're very kind."

"Why don't you go home?" Jacques suggested, after a few more minutes of strained silence. It was a strange situation, we didn't seem to have anything to say to each other. "Don't feel you have to stay. I'm all right, I promise you."

I got up, almost thankfully.

"Are you sure there's nothing you need?" I enquired hesitantly, guilt feelings at my desire to leave welling up in me.

"Nothing at all," he smiled. "Food's out. I'm on some sort of diet."

"What about books?"

He hesitated before replying, obviously searching for the right words.

"I don't feel much like reading," he said quietly. "But if I do think of anything I'll get the nurse to telephone you."

"Yes, do that," I answered. "I'll ring tonight to find out how you are and I'll come back to see you tomorrow."

I should have seen the warning light. Jacques not wanting to read, something must be very wrong. Books were his greatest pleasure and he had often jokingly said he'd love a few days in hospital just to have time to catch up on his reading. And now he had the time, and he didn't want to. But I didn't get the message.

He took my hand as I bent to kiss his forehead.

"God bless you, darling," he said softly. "And don't worry, I'll be home in a few days."

With so much calm optimism around me I took it all at face value and, for the time being, didn't worry.

Each afternoon I went in to see him and each evening I returned home to the buzzing of the telephone. It had not taken long for the news to travel along the church grapevine and even that first evening my loving Christian friends were on the line sympathising with me, encouraging me and offering to help in any way possible.

After the first few days, I accepted the numerous invitations to meals which were showered on me and, as I was not unduly worried about Jacques' health, began to enjoy this new freedom and importance I had slipped into through no fault of my own. Everyone was so kind and wherever I went there was a deference, like that shown to some very important person who suddenly comes into a room, a sudden lull in the conversation while people gathered round to hear what I had to say. We were really headlines in our church community at that time; Jacques was very much loved and I was cashing in on his popularity and, in a macabre way, enjoying it.

Until that afternoon when I arrived late at the hospital to find that they had been trying to get hold of me for hours. Before seeing Jacques; I was ushered in to see his consultant who told me that although they had tried to avoid surgery there had been a turn for the worse and they would have to operate – and quickly. It was Wednesday and Jacques was to be taken for examinations to another Paris hospital with a team specialising in heart surgery and operated on on the Friday.

It was a dreadful shock and it brought me to my senses ... and to my knees. As I returned home in the darkness, numbed and frightened, I knew that this time I had really come back to an empty house.

I wonder how God put up with me! Just as he thought I had at last understood, up popped another sin which blinded my vision. I was a Christian, totally committed to him, still into my Bible and my prayer life, but still open to any attack the devil cared to make – and he knew my weak points so much better than I did and had no scruples about creeping up and hitting me from behind. Now I had fallen again into his flattery trap, that deadly trap of pride the worst of all the sins because it opens the door to indifference and so many others.

The next afternoon our dear friend and chaplain, Alan Lindsay,* came to the hospital to give communion to both

* Now Canon Alan Lindsay, chaplain of St John and St Philip's church in The Hague.

Jacques and me. He was gentle and kind and understanding, but it was a difficult task as the nurses didn't seem to grasp what was happening and throughout the short service kept bursting in and out. What should have been a quiet time with Jesus to give us strength for the next day turned into a stop-start affair. I ended up crying on Alan's sympathetic shoulder; I couldn't help letting the tears flow and Jacques, in his weakness, tried to comfort me.

What I didn't then know was that the surgeon had told Jacques that he had a fifty-fifty chance of survival so he had written me a letter to be posted should he not come through the operation. I don't think he expected to live and my apparent indifference to his condition during the past two weeks must have hurt him deeply. But he didn't say anything. He thought about me and asked if there was anyone who could be with me so that I needn't be alone on the Friday morning. I knew there were plenty of people who would willingly have stayed with me, but I felt it had to be someone very special with whom I could be myself, as by now I, too, understood the full implications of this surgery.

And then I saw once again how wonderfully the Lord works, how he plans and directs our lives, weaving the tapestry in and out down to the minutest detail as my brother, Geoffrey's, name suddenly flashed into my mind.

Ever since I married, my brother and I had lived in different countries. As children and adolescents, we had always been very close but for years we had never been within visiting distance. Yet last autumn he and his family had settled in Normandy, only one hundred kilometres from us. Of course, Geoffrey was the one to be with me, perhaps the only person with whom I would not have to pretend. I thanked God for this strange "coincidence" which had so recently brought us close to each other again.

I also thanked God for my wonderful family, as it was not the first time Geoffrey and his wife Sylvie had stepped in in an emergency. During my two months away after my breakdown, they had lovingly taken a bewildered Yves and brought a smile and reassurance back to him as he romped and played with his cousins in their home in Germany.

Now, once again, a telephone call brought Geoffrey to my side and on that never-to-be-forgotten Friday morning whilst I travelled across Paris in the ambulance with my husband, my brother followed in his car. It was a long day. There were all sorts of tests to be made, and I remember sitting in a narrow corridor for hours on end knowing nothing, just interminably waiting, listening to the noises coming from behind the closed door through which Jacques' trolley had been wheeled. My brother had had to remain upstairs, so I was alone. It was one of those rare days we so often get in Paris in early February, soft and balmy, a flash of summer which gives us hope but does not last, and the long windows opposite where I was sitting must have been south-facing because I can remember the hot sun pouring in and making me drowsy as I sat there, hour after hour, with nothing to do but wait.

At last someone came through the door and sat down beside me. It was the surgeon, his face was strong and kind and I liked him immediately.

"The examination has shown us we can't postpone the operation," he said quietly, and considerately went on to explain why. But the words didn't mean much to me and I just nodded dumbly.

"He's been taken to a room on the seventh floor. Go up and sit with him for a while, but he's very tired so don't be upset if he doesn't feel like talking."

I went up to sit with Jacques. Far from talking, there didn't seem to be anything to say and after a little while the nurses came to prepare him for the operation and I went and sat in the little waiting room at the end of the corridor until someone should tell me what else to do. I felt like a chess pawn on a board being moved from place to place, waiting for someone to pick me up and put me in the next position.

My brother appeared.

"Come on," he said firmly, "you've got to have something to eat. It's gone three o'clock and you've had nothing all day."

So this was the next move. But I shook my head.

"I'm not hungry," I replied, "I'd rather sit and wait."

"*I'll* wait," said Geoffrey, taking hold of my arm. "There's a restaurant right outside the hospital gate. Go over there and have lunch. You can't go on like this."

Obediently, I took the lift and walked out into the soft

warm air; everything around me seemed to be dancing in the sunshine, in stark contrast to my mood. Entering the restaurant, which had now emptied of its lunchtime crowd, I looked blankly at the menu, anxious about being away from the hospital too long. When the waiter appeared I hurriedly ordered coffee and *tartines*, the quickest thing possible. He looked at me in surprise, then shrugged his shoulders; perhaps he was used to mesmerised customers coming straight from the hospital asking for breakfast at three thirty in the afternoon. I drank the scalding brew, gobbled the bread and in fifteen minutes was back at my post.

Geoffrey and I sat in silence for another hour. Nothing seemed to be happening, but it was when he went off to telephone Sylvie that the nurse put her head round the waiting room door.

"Your husband is going down to the theatre now," she said brightly. "Perhaps you'd like to say goodbye to him."

My heart leapt; it sounded so final – "say goodbye".

"Here's his glasses and his wedding ring," she went on. "You may as well take them, he won't be needing them."

Did she mean to stab me? The words were spoken casually, but to me they were fraught with meaning. If only she had said, "he won't be needing them for the time being" or "for the next few days" but, "he won't be needing them" full stop, added to that "goodbye", spelt disaster to my tired brain.

As she turned away, I saw the trolley coming down the corridor towards the lift and it seemed at that moment as if my life also turned away, away from the happy, comfortable routine I had known and taken for granted during all those years of marriage. And I faced a void, a nothingness, a terrible emptiness, at the centre of which loomed the stark realisation that before the day was over I might be a widow.

Nothing seemed real any more and I clung desperately to Jesus. He did not fail me. I felt a deep, overwhelming peace flood through me and I knew that I was safe in his arms, that he would keep me and protect me and carry me over the yawning chasm which was threatening to swallow me up. I went steadily towards the trolley and walked beside it as far as the lift, holding Jacques' hand. Then the doors closed noiselessly behind him and I was alone again in the stark

white brilliance of that antiseptic corridor, with only the
pungent smell of disinfectant to remind me of where I was.

Geoffrey returned and took me home. He wanted to stay
with me but I assured him that I was going to bed and there
was no need; I'd feel happier if he went back to his family.
My brother was a housemaster at L'Ecole des Roches, a
large English-style boarding school in Normandy, and I
knew how difficult it must be for Sylvie and the house
matron to be left to cope on their own with forty-eight boys
between twelve and eighteen. He took one look at my face
and decided there was no point in insisting, so I watched his
car drive off into the darkness and then walked wearily back
into the house, not quite knowing what to do.

It was eight o'clock and I had been up since five. The most
sensible thing would have been to go to bed, but instead I
wandered around from room to room, picking things up and
putting them down again. Jesus had given me his peace there
in that hospital corridor and it was still with me, otherwise I
would not have been able to let my brother go, but would
have clung to him for comfort and support. At the same
time, he had also given me another insight into myself and
my perplexed feelings and, between us, my Lord and I were
balancing the accounts.

Taking my Bible, I sat down in the drawing-room in front
of the dead ashes. The room was cold and although it would
have changed everything to throw a few logs into the
fireplace and make a blaze, I couldn't be bothered; it seemed
pointless to do it for myself. And once again Jesus said:

"Do you see what I mean?"

And I felt his gentle gaze upon me.

I did see what he meant, only too well. How often in the
past had I spent my time with "if onlys" – if only I could have
a little peace, if only I could have the house to myself, if only
I could have one day when there was no one around. Oh yes,
I could see what he meant!

"When you belong to me," he continued, "I am able to
show you that so often the things you sigh for are not what
you really want and you are not always happy when you get
them. How often people are grateful for the prayers I didn't
answer, or answered by 'no'."

The hall clock struck eleven and I went to the telephone.

"He's not back yet," said a cool voice on the other end of the line.

"Not *back*?" I echoed hollowly.

"Ring in the morning, around eight thirty," came the professional tones.

I replaced the receiver and that icy grip took hold of my heart again.

I want you to trust me in your times of trouble, so that I can rescue you, and you can give me glory.
(Psalm 50: 15) (The Living Bible)

17

NEVER LOSE HOPE

As I tossed and turned, unable to sleep, I thought the morning would never come but it did and, to my surprise, it caught me unawares. I must have dozed off with the dawn and when I awoke the room was light and the bedside clock pointed to eight thirty-five.

Hurriedly I picked up the receiver.

"Yes," came the same professional voice, "the operation was successful but your husband is about to go down to the theatre again – there's something not quite right."

"But..." I stammered, unable to believe what I was hearing.

"Don't come to see him before this afternoon," she cut in, "after three o'clock. He should be round then."

"But why..." I cried.

"The surgeon will explain when you come," said the brisk, matter-of-fact voice.

I wanted to shout:

"It's my husband you're talking about, not a name on a bed chart. Tell me what's happened. I *must* know."

But the click told me that she had hung up and I felt it was pointless to ring back.

When I entered the hospital that Saturday afternoon, I had no idea what to expect. Hope had kept me buoyant during the day... and my authoritative prayers!

"He's doing your work, Lord," I had repeated over and over again. "You know how much he loves you, how much there still is to do. It's unthinkable that you should call him home now."

No, I told myself confidently, God can't do that, he needs Jacques here. Jacques had become a Gideon a few years earlier, a member of that Christian Businessmen's Association which distributes Bibles to hotel rooms and hospital wards and gives them out to schoolchildren, university students, prisoners and members of the Armed Forces. The group had only been established in France within the last decade and had very few members for the work to be done, and my husband had thrown himself whole-heartedly into this new venture for the Lord. Most of his spare time went in trying to further the efforts of the Association in France; he was needed, God knew that, there was no question of his work being finished, God had made a mistake. Once again, I was telling my Maker what to do.

As the lift stopped at the seventh floor and I walked out into that white corridor, the nurse at the desk came towards me. She was the one who had been on duty the night before and I was grateful not to have to face the one with the brisk tone who had answered my calls.

"The surgeon would like to see you," she said and disappeared into a room, leaving me standing in the corridor. I peeped in and saw two men in long white coats looking at dots on a TV screen, then the older of the two got up and came towards me, and I recognised him as the man who had inspired such confidence in me the day before.

He cleared his throat before he spoke.

"I'm afraid the operation didn't go exactly as we had expected," he said, and paused, obviously wondering what my reaction would be.

I looked at him and he went into a lot of technical details which were way above my head: it was years since I had trained as a nurse and everything was different. I didn't understand a word of what he was saying; all I gathered was that he was finding it difficult to tell me that, perhaps, after all, my husband would not come through.

I bit my lip and looked at the floor as he paused again.

"Are you trying to tell me my husband is dying?" I asked flatly.

Perhaps he was taken aback by my direct question because he didn't answer immediately. I felt sorry for this man who had tried so hard and yet had only grim news to report. As the white walls began to spin around me, through the haze I heard the surgeon's voice.

"We must never lose hope," he said quietly, and turned away.

Nurses passed to and fro as I remained standing, bewildered, in that stark corridor, trying to understand what I had just heard. It was all a bad dream, this must be happening to someone else. Jacques couldn't be dying, he couldn't leave me, there must be some mistake, my husband had always been so healthy, never ill, really ill, until now ... until now; the words echoed round and round in my head, somehow mingling with those the surgeon had left unspoken. As the truth slowly sank in, an icy flood poured through my whole body and, like a drowning man, I clung to the fact that there is always hope.

Mechanically I put on the sterile gown and mask the nurse was holding out and went to my husband's bedside. I had never seen a patient after an open heart operation, that kind of surgery came long after my time, and I was totally unprepared for the sight which greeted me.

Jacques lay still and seemingly lifeless on a narrow bed, another television screen with dots racing across it by his side. His limp arms were stretched out as if on a cross and it was impossible to get near him because of the apparatus dangling all around. There was a terrible burning sensation in my throat and I felt as if I were going to suffocate. This was not my husband, the quiet, confident rock I had always leaned on. This creature from outer space was not even human. Jacques must have sensed my presence in the room because his short-sighted hazel eyes half-opened and his mouth moved as if he understood my horror and revulsion and wanted to speak to reassure me. But no words came and, as his eyelids fluttered momentarily and then dropped, the nurse took my arm and led me away.

I stumbled out of the hospital into the shimmering afternoon sunshine. It was another beautiful day, but the only sight which mimed grotesquely before my eyes was my husband's lifeless shape on that narrow bed. Broken and afraid I reached the car park, wrenched open the door and crumpled against the steering wheel, sobbing helplessly.

Then anger took over.

"God," I cried in rage, "how could you do this to us? He's your child, you didn't have to put him through all that. Why didn't you let him die yesterday, on the operating table, or two weeks ago?"

Lights were beginning to pop up in the shops and houses

as I wended my way home, down the narrow streets jostling with the happy Saturday evening crowds. But their laughter merely accentuated my utter desolation and I wondered bleakly what tomorrow would bring, whether anything would ever be the same again.

Words a friend had said to me when she heard of Jacques' illness hammered incessantly in my brain:

"But he's been looking so tired for such a long time. Hadn't you noticed?"

I hadn't, and I wondered deep inside, or perhaps it was just to excuse myself, whether, had the positions been reversed, he would have noticed had it happened to me. We had taken each other for granted in a comfortable kind of way. He was my husband, I loved him, I knew he loved me and he was always there when I needed him. Until now.

How had it happened? I looked back over the months, but there was no explanation. He had been working hard but then so had everyone else's husband who had a job with responsibility. But I should have noticed his tiredness. Guilt wracked me mercilessly.

The telephone was ringing as I entered the hall.

"Have you any news?" came a hesitant voice.

I felt very much for our friends at this time. They were so good about keeping in touch and wanting to help, but what was there that anyone could do... except pray, and they didn't all realise how important this was.

"Not really," I answered brightly. "I've just got back from the hospital and saw him for a couple of minutes but, of course, he's very tired and it will be a day or two before he's feeling better."

We exchanged a few more platitudes and I put the receiver down, and the endless evening hours stretched in front of me. It was no use going back to the hospital. They had said it would be difficult to give me any news for another twenty-four hours, but had promised to telephone if there was any change – either way.

That "either way" struck terror in my heart. There were only two ways – either Jacques would recover... or he would not. What if it were the wrong way?

The telephone rang again, and I seemed to be moving about in a vacuum, nothing was real.

"He's just the same," I answered brightly once more. "No, I'm perfectly all right. Please don't worry. Of course I'm not lonely. I've got masses to do and anyway I want to stay around in case the hospital rings ... they said they would if there were any change. Have a good evening, love to Roger, see you in church in the morning."

And I dropped the receiver in place, wondering what the masses of things were that I had to do.

Why had I suddenly become such a liar? Why didn't I say:

"I'm feeling wretched, I'm desperately lonely, the house is desolate and I can't stand being here on my own."

They were my friends, my Christian friends, they only wanted to help. Although I had wanted to burst into tears as soon as I heard the concern in their voices and felt their love even over the telephone, I had turned all hard and metallic and brittle, replying like an answering machine.

I slowly turned my husband's wedding ring round and round on my finger: it was far too big but I had placed it between my engagement and my own wedding ring when the nurse had handed it to me.

The telephone rang again.

They only want to help. They only want to help. They only want to help. Like a train thundering over the rails, the words went hammering through my brain. Let them comfort you. What makes you think you're so strong?

I lifted the receiver again and from far off heard my answering voice.

"No, of course not, I'm perfectly all right. Don't worry. I'll see you in the morning."

I put down the phone and realised as I snapped on the light that I had to do something with my time or go to pieces and ... the children needed me.

By midnight, when I rang the hospital again, my house was the cleanest in the district. All the curtains had been torn down and washed and the furniture frantically polished through the long evening hours. This time, a sympathetic voice answered my call.

"He's just the same," she said. "Go to bed and try to get some sleep. I promise to ring you if there is any change."

My whole body was aching and crying out for rest but I knew that sleep was far away. As I sat down in the chilly drawing-room, the Lord suddenly brought back to my mind lines from *To Live Again*, the book in which Catherine Marshall describes her feelings when her husband Peter had been taken to hospital after a heart attack and she had found herself alone and afraid on a dark January night. She had found peace by giving Peter to Jesus, taking her hands off him and leaving him in God's hands. I was able to identify with her and remembered how she had finally given up praying for healing and had just surrendered her husband, given him back to Jesus, saying she was willing to accept our Lord's decision for Peter's life.

Some brittle cord snapped within me and I felt the waves of resistance which I had built up to the outside world, to my friends, to the will of God during these last fifteen days, come pouring over me and gush away, leaving me limp and cleansed. And I knew that if one of my loving friends rang at that moment, asking for news, they would receive a very different reply. I would no longer say:

"I'm perfectly all right. Don't worry about me."

I would have stretched out my arms to them over the telephone wires and said:

"Come, I need you. I need the comfort of another human being. I need someone to hold my hand, to cry on. I need someone to pray with me."

The barriers were down, the mask had dropped and in a flash I saw my earthly pride, my image, dissolve and leave me naked and defenceless. But it was past midnight and I knew that no one would call.

I sank to my knees, resting my forehead against the comfortable old wing chair, as I had done years earlier on that pearly May morning when I gave my heart to Jesus.

"Loving Heavenly Father," I breathed, "forgive me."

And then no words came.

As I knelt in the cold, silent room, my face buried in my husband's favourite armchair, I felt a presence beside me, and I lifted my head. A silver streak of light was shining in through the undrawn curtains: it fell on to the piano and my eyes were drawn to a piece of music propped up above the keys. It was a hymn book and in the darkened room the moonlight clearly pinpointed two titles. The first was "Give to the winds your fears" and, opposite it, "God will take care of you".

I caught my breath and my hands gripped the arm of the chair. I had vaguely heard of the second hymn but the first was completely unknown to me. I hadn't touched the piano since Jacques was taken ill: how could those titles, so full of meaning, have got there? And my heart almost broke within me as the full significance of the words struck home. God was clearly telling me that he was in control, that I was in his care and had nothing to fear, and as he did so the moonlight slowly drifted across the top of the piano until it fell upon a smiling photo of Jacques and the children taken only a few months before.

Peace and hope suddenly surged through me and words came tumbling from my lips.

"Father," I cried, "oh loving Father, he's yours. I place him unconditionally in your hands, knowing that your plan is the perfect plan for our lives. And if, tonight, the time has come for Jacques to go home, I give him back to you. Only help me truly to give my fears to the winds and rest in you."

As I rose from my knees the room was again in darkness, the moonlight had gone. But my fears had gone too. I had surrendered my burden and Jesus had taken it from me and given me his peace. And, as I went slowly towards the stairs, I knew that he would also give me sleep.

I am with you; that is all you need. My power shows up best in weak people.
(2 Corinthians 12: 9) (The Living Bible)

A SONG OF TRIUMPH

As my mind slowly surfaced, groping its way back to consciousness after a night of deep, refreshing sleep, I heard the bells from the old village church ringing the Angelus. Completely at peace, I leant over towards the telephone beside my bed and picked up the receiver.

"Your husband has had a good night," came the sterile reply.

It was the terse, businesslike nurse on the line again, but I didn't care. My heart leapt for joy as I replaced the receiver and fell out of bed on to my knees, feeling nothing but an immense peace.

And as I knelt by my bedside, lost in love and adoration, my heart winging out on tumultuous waves of joy to meet my saviour, the God in whom I had put my whole trust and to whom I had abandoned everything, unknown words began to flow from my tongue; words of praise and thanksgiving in a beautiful new language.

I had heard about the gifts of the Spirit, had read about "speaking in tongues" and tossed it off, as everyone does who has not experienced the gift, as unimportant and unnecessary. But that morning, as these joyous sounds surged from my lips and flew heavenwards, I knew it was not unimportant, that it was, for me, the culmination of long years of climbing. I had finally reached the summit, come into his presence and, because of this new language which Jesus had given me, had the assurance that his Holy Spirit dwelled within me.

And I knew that this new tongue was to me the most important thing which had happened in my Christian walk and that from the summit which I had now attained I could fly off to other heights, other gifts, knowing that in my heart

I had his precious spirit to guide me, to teach me, to lead me. To receive from my Lord a new language in which to praise him was the lowliest and yet for me the most powerful gift, because from now onwards I could really intercede as he wanted me to, really "speak with the tongues of men and of angels". I could pray in the Spirit with groanings too deep for words.

As I knelt there I suddenly realised that, mingled with the glorious pealing of the church bells, was the insistent ringing of the telephone by my bedside and, coming back down to earth, I picked up the receiver.

The voice of the lovely Christian girl Hervé was later to marry came down the line.

"Hervé will be with you any minute," she announced.

I gasped, knowing how precious time was for his studies: he had so much backlog to make up.

"He'll be there for breakfast," Cécile told me.

It was as well that she had rung because I had hardly replaced the receiver before I heard noises in the kitchen below.

"Hervé," I called, going to the top of the stairs.

"No, it's me," came my brother's voice. "Hervé's here. We're just making breakfast."

I couldn't believe it. Yesterday I had been so alone and now the house was swarming with people. I put on a dressing-gown and went downstairs.

"What are you both doing here?" I marvelled.

"We've come to see you," Geoffrey grinned. "Here, sit down, breakfast's ready."

"You shouldn't have come," I said, lamely.

"I knew you'd say that," Hervé smiled. "That's why I asked Cécile to ring you *after* I'd left."

He looked at me intently.

"Why didn't you let me know earlier?" he asked quietly.

I bit my lip.

"I didn't want you to be worried," I said at last. "You've got so much work to make up."

Hervé bent and kissed my cheek.

"I know you meant well," he said gently. "But my father is more important than my studies."

I sat down, not knowing what to say.

"When did you arrive?" I asked, looking up.

"A few minutes ago," he replied, pouring out my coffee. "And *you*?"

I looked accusingly at my brother, knowing how busy weekends at the school were for him.

"Late last night," he answered. "The house was in darkness so I jumped the wall and your wonderful watchdogs didn't even bark. Now, stop worrying: Sylvie's coping splendidly and she didn't mind a bit."

"You're both very naughty," I said quietly, and added, "but very sweet."

As I walked into church that Sunday morning, flanked by my two men, the service was just beginning. To my surprise, it was being taped and dedicated to Jacques. Our little church in Versailles shared Alan Lindsay with the sister church of Holy Trinity at Maisons-Lafitte and this was the alternate Sunday when a lay reader took the service. It was Michael Haworth, a retired naval captain and the friend to whom Jacques had given the letter which I was to receive should he not survive. Michael spoke so warmly and so movingly about my husband, praying for his complete recovery and thanking God for having kept him safe so far. When it came to the closing hymn, he said very simply:

"This is Jacques' favourite, so let's make it a rousing song of triumph because, don't forget, he'll be hearing it."

We sang heartily, the tears pricking my eyes, and, as I looked around at all those dear friends who had been such a support and comfort to me during the past two weeks, I saw many a wet cheek and handkerchiefs being surreptitiously slid beneath damp spectacles.

It was a beautiful service and when it ended our friends clustered round us. This time there was no vicarious pleasure for me in the attention I was indirectly receiving because of my husband's illness, only a feeling of gratitude for the love with which I was surrounded and deep humility that we should be so showered with blessings.

We went to the hospital again that afternoon, but only I was allowed to see Jacques. This time I was prepared for all the apparatus and even thought he looked better than the day before. The surgeon said he was holding his own, but otherwise was non-committal.

For another forty-eight hours his life still hung in the balance, then slowly he began to improve...

Bee arrived home the next day with her diploma in her pocket. The course in England had ended and, suddenly, the house was full of life again. I remember taking her in to see Jacques the day after she arrived and turning round to see her standing horrified in the doorway, tears streaming down into the mask over her mouth. And I realised how quickly I had become accustomed to the Intensive Care Unit and how little I had prepared her for the change in the smiling father who had so recently waved her goodbye.

In March, when Yves and Christopher came home for their half-term break, Jacques was sitting up in an armchair in a hospital room of his own. The boys had been told, at school, that their father was ill but I hadn't considered it necessary to give them a lot of details which at nine and twelve I thought they could not possibly understand. But since then I have often wondered if I was right to keep them apart from something so very vital, and queried the way we try to shield children from death, preventing them from attending the funeral of a beloved grandparent or stemming our tears so that they don't see us cry. And were I to live those months over again, I think I would have tried to explain to them a little more of the drama which was rocking our family.

Once more our friends rallied round and that half-term weekend the boys were invited out and kept so busy that they hardly had time to notice Jacques' absence. On the Monday afternoon when I took them to the hospital to say goodbye to their father before they caught their plane back to England, Jacques was again propped in his armchair. And, as we sat chatting, Yves suddenly got up and, gently pulling at his father's pyjama jacket, stared inside at the wad of dressing on his chest. Then, without comment, he turned away.

Jacques and I looked at each other, not knowing what to say, but it was time to go so I took advantage of the bustle of their departure not to broach the subject. I still don't know what prompted Yves to do that, or what went through his mind, whether fear, or pain, or even mere curiosity, and again I wish now that I had been more open with them.

Christopher was still a "baby" with his head full of nothing but rugger and pranks, but Yves was sensitive and mature and felt things more deeply.

As he waved them goodbye, Jacques promised to see them in England on the last day of term when Yves was to be confirmed in the school chapel. We were both very much looking forward to being there and, being a very easy patient, Jacques had made good progress. There did not seem any reason at the time why he should not make the journey.

But a week beforehand, he began to have pain in his chest wound and an abscess was discovered where the stitches had been. After trying in vain to reduce the angry red swelling with medication, the doctors concluded the only alternative was surgery. So, regretfully, Jacques went back into Intensive Care to prepare for his return to the operating theatre.

Once again, my brother was by my side and I had further reason to bless my sister-in-law who had been so loving and understanding during this traumatic time, when she yet again took over her husband's duties at the school for a few days whilst he accompanied me to England. Ironically, at the time when my father, my brother, my nephew and I entered the little school chapel for this important event in Yves' spiritual life, Jacques was taken down to the theatre for his third operation.

Yves had been invited to spend Easter with friends in Norfolk and Geoffrey and Sylvie were taking Christopher down to St Raphael with them. Christopher adored being with his three cousins and usually could not wait to go to them but, when we got back to Paris and I began sorting out the clothes he would need for the beach, he clung to me and cried.

"Mummy," he sobbed, "I don't want to go. I want to stay with you."

I couldn't understand it and tried to comfort him, telling him what a lovely time he was going to have by the sea, but he just continued to sob quietly and I didn't know what to do. My spirits were already at zero; the thought of spending Easter, usually such a happy, family time, alone had only been made bearable because I knew that the boys would be enjoying themselves.

Geoffrey and Pascal, his eleven-year-old son, managed to prise Christopher away and jolly him up saying, quite rightly I suppose, that he would be all right once they set off; and finally they left, my son's chubby, tear-stained face gazing miserably out of the back window as the car sped up the hill and out of sight.

It was Good Friday and the promise of spring which we had had in February seemed to have been completely forgotten. The weather was cold and damp, I was tired and began to cough as I went back into the house and prepared to visit Jacques. The operation had been successful, but he was still in the Intensive Care Unit.

That night I coughed even more and when I went back to the hospital the next afternoon I realised that the last thing my husband needed was my germs on top of everything else, so when the nurse suggested it would be wiser not to visit him until I felt better, I went home to bed feeling lost and lonely and sorry for myself.

Easter Sunday dawned, dull and windy, and I hacked my way through the day. Nearly all my friends were away and the hours dragged endlessly. After lunch on the following Tuesday I could stand it no longer and got out of bed and went to the hospital to see Jacques. He was his usual bright, cheerful self and he cheered me up, but two days later they took out the stitches... and the wound broke open again.

Although I didn't know it then, this was to be the pattern of our life for the next two years, hopes being fulfilled and then dashed.

Just before the boys returned to school at the end of April, Jacques was allowed home and the excitement in our house that morning was frenetic! They cut up old sheets and painted greetings on them, making them into streamers and banners to hang from every window, each one reading "Welcome Home Daddy" in different colours. But the Daddy who came home was not the Daddy who had played football and swam with them only a few months earlier. He was a weak, sick man who walked like a monkey, arms dangling forwards because of the wound and the constant pain in his chest. And the boys soon learned that life was not going to be the same as before and, mentally, they backed away.

Two days before they left, they had a party in the garden

and half-way through I felt a sudden irritation with Bee who was supposed to be helping and had completely disappeared. Angrily I went upstairs to her room. She was lying on the bed twisted with pain... and all the signs of an acute appendicitis. That was just about the final straw!

It was Saturday afternoon and our own doctor was away, so I decided the easiest thing to do was to bundle her into the car and take her to the local hospital. But what about the fourteen little boys who were racing around and would create havoc if left unattended? Jacques was in no state to cope and once again I knew the strength of Christian friends and the love which allows one to call on them in the most impossible situations and know that they will willingly take over. I drove Bee to the hospital and within an hour she was in bed, sedated and prepared for an emergency operation.

Christopher and Yves left on Monday morning; on Wednesday, Jacques returned to the hospital in Paris for a fourth operation in yet another attempt to close the gaping wound in his chest and as I skated madly backwards and forwards between my two patients I felt I was being pulled in all directions.

I don't honestly know how I coped during those early days of May 1975. Had I not known that Jesus was with me, that there are no accidents in his perfect plan for our lives, I think I would have succumbed to self-pity always one of my strong points. But, in spite of everything, I carried within me this deep assurance that he was there beside me, that his hand was guiding my life, although at times it seemed as if the boat was rocking and tossing so badly in the storm that it could not but capsize.

Although I had chosen my Master I had not chosen my road and the truth of the words "when you don't feel like praying, *that* is the time to pray" struck home. The wonderful gift Jesus had given me the morning after my total surrender of my husband to him was a precious boon to me: when I didn't know how to pray, the Spirit intervened and prayed for me with "groanings too deep for words". He also praised for me and, as I prayed, I would find that I was raising my face to heaven and my arms were lifted up in praise and I rose from my knees renewed with fresh hope and joy and peace.

Bee was discharged from hospital and came home to convalesce. Not long afterwards Jacques arrived too, but as Bee grew stronger and the colour returned to her cheeks, it was obvious that the reverse was happening to him. His wound had broken open again even before he left the hospital and in the months which followed, as he gradually became weaker, we went from doctor to doctor, from allergy specialist to homeopath in an attempt to find a solution. But there was none, and this gaping, suppurating wound had to be dressed twice a day. The following February, in desperation, he went back into the hospital and they operated again, but with no result and, this time, they told us there was nothing more they could do.

So he came home and, one evening in October, Alan Lindsay and his wife Catherine came with other members of the little Anglican congregation of St Mark's, Versailles, and we had a laying-on of hands service for Jacques in our drawing-room. It was very simple, but very moving. Alan read from James' Letter and claimed the promise of healing and, when it was over, Jacques, whose deep, steady faith, unlike mine, had never wavered or doubted during all these trials, smiled up at the group of friends clustered round him.

"I know I'll be healed," he said quietly. "Jesus has promised. If he doesn't take the disease away from me, then he'll take me away from the disease. Whichever way he chooses, I'm wholly at peace."

And, having placed himself in his Saviour's loving arms, he awaited the Lord's decision.

It did not come immediately.

More months of pain and weakness went by and somehow we just lived from day to day. Jacques remained serene and hopeful, but I was often despondent and, as my spirits flagged, it was he, the sick man, who supported and comforted me. Looking back, we might have been alone on a desert island at that time. We lived the life of the recluse. If ever I accepted an invitation, I usually ended up going alone as Jacques was rarely well enough to accompany me so, in the end, we stopped accepting and lived in a little cocoon of our own, just us and the Lord.

Then one Sunday evening in the spring of 1977, over two years after the first operation and more than a year since the doctors had said they could do no more for him, we went to a service held by "Teen Challenge". They were very active in Paris at that time, with their coffee bars for young people and drop-outs and their rehabilitation centre for drug addicts, and the room, rather like a warehouse which they rented in the Latin Quarter, was always full of people of all nationalities and from all walks of life for the Sunday evening service.

Jacques and I went occasionally and had got to know Bill Williams who was pastor at the time* and many of the regular members who had become our friends and had prayed for us during our critical time. As we arrived, Jacques stopped to look at the book stall and I went in on my own and bumped into Bill in the doorway. He had just returned to Paris after three months' absence and was not taking the service that evening.

"How's your husband?" he enquired.

"Oh, he's fine," I replied.

It was far from true, but I had got tired of saying that he was no better or even worse; it put the questioner in an awkward position and he didn't know where to go from there. So we had decided that we would merely tell everyone who asked, except our immediate circle, that everything was going well, even though we knew the reverse to be true.

At the end of the service, Bill got up to talk a little about his trip and say how pleased he was to be back. Then he suddenly said:

"I feel there is someone here this evening who is in need of healing. The secret of answered prayer is praise, so let's praise the Lord and pray for him or her."

Bill must have been very sensitive to the Holy Spirit's leading that evening because I don't ever remember his having done such a thing before. Maybe he had, but it certainly was not his custom. Jacques and I were both surprised and wondered who that person in need of healing could be.

My husband seemed very thoughtful on the journey home but, as we were watching the late-night news before going to

* He is now principal of the Continental Bible College in Brussels.

bed, he said:

"Something very strange happened to me during that healing prayer. I suddenly began to shake uncontrollably and felt as if an electric current were going through my chest."

For a moment I didn't take in what he was saying, then quickly went over to him and began to loosen his bandages.

The wound was exactly the same.

But the next morning I heard Jacques get up and go into the bathroom early. I felt a vague irritation at being half-roused from my comfortable oblivion. It was Monday and it was raining hard. I didn't want to face the day. So when I felt my husband gently shaking me awake before the alarm clock had rung, my irritation turned to exasperation at being cheated out of precious sleep.

Jacques was sitting on the side of the bed.

"I've something to show you," he said, turning me towards him.

I angrily opened one eye, then blinked and abruptly sat up. My husband was wearing only pyjama trousers. His chest was bare... and clean.

Jacques smiled down at me as I put out my hand unbelievingly and gingerly touched him. But it was true: there on his chest where for two years had been a messy, leaking wound was a long, clean, pink scar.

We looked at each other and for a few minutes neither of us spoke. I don't think we really believed what had happened. I know I didn't. But then the glorious truth suddenly dawned on us: Jesus had touched his sick body and made him whole, just as the Bible had promised he would.

I had read those words so many times and heard them preached from the pulpit and even though I had experienced Christ's presence and power in my life, miracles, rather like death, were something that happened to other people. But now I realised that a miracle had happened to us, to our family, and I remembered Jesus' words:

"When the Holy Spirit comes upon you, you will do even greater miracles than I."

And I got out of bed feeling very humble, but very grateful for the faith of one man who believed strongly enough and had dared to claim this power so that Christ's healing could flow into my husband's sick body and make him whole.

Believers will be given the power to perform miracles: they
will drive out demons in my name... they will place their
hands on sick people, who will get well.
(Mark 16: 17) (Good News Bible)

19

THE CLIMAX

For several days Jacques and I were very quiet; this miracle which had come as a thunderbolt into our lives when we least expected it and had almost stopped hoping for it, had struck with such force that we had been left gasping and speechless. We had this living proof before us in that bright, pink, clean scar and yet it was too much to take in all at once and, inwardly, I am sure each of us thought that we would soon wake up and discover that it was just a beautiful dream. So we were unwilling to become too involved and face the truth of what had actually happened in our lives.

On the following Saturday morning, I went into the bathroom to find Jacques standing in front of the mirror, chest bare, gently wiping his scar with spirit preparatory to putting on the bandages and I suddenly realised the absurdity of the situation. Jesus had touched him, had answered months and months of anguished prayers and petitions not only from us but from Christian friends all over, and now that these prayers had been beautifully answered we, in our finite state, refused to believe that the miracle had happened.

I stood looking at him. He turned and faced me, then looked away.

"You don't have to do that, you know," I said gently, taking the bottle of spirit from his hand. "You don't have to wear bandages any more... you're healed."

"I know," he said simply.

"Then why *are* you doing it?" I insisted.

He shrugged his shoulders.

"I don't know," he answered helplessly. "I just feel safer with the bandages on, that's all."

I understood his feelings. For over two years he had

looked like a pouter pigeon, his chest packed tight. And if ever he had omitted to clean and dress his wound at night, the next morning blood and pus had leaked through on to his pyjamas, and he was obviously afraid that the same thing would happen again. I took the cotton wool from his hand.

"Try it," I said. "Just leave the bandages off for today. You're not going anywhere. Even if your shirt gets messed up, it doesn't matter."

He said nothing, but he did not resist. And he did not have an "accident"; how could he, there was no longer any wound to leak? He has never put a dressing on his chest since.

I think that was when we both really grasped the joyous, incredible truth, the wonderful truth, that he was healed, and we suddenly wanted to laugh and shout and tell everyone we met. But Jacques was still weak and I wondered how far the healing would go. Could it be too much to hope that Jesus had healed him completely, from the pain, the weakness, not just the leaking wound, and truly made him whole again?

Once again, I was underestimating the Master. When Jesus heals he does not do it by halves and within three weeks Jacques was a new man. From being an invalid who had been unable to turn over in bed or put on his jacket unaided because of the pain in his chest, the man for whom the doctors could do no more began to dig the garden, run in the woods with the dogs and, that joyous Easter when Christopher came home from school, to kick a football with him in the park.

A month after his healing, Jacques asked if he might say a few words in church and when he stood in front of the congregation, upright and smiling, the greyness in his face replaced by a healthy glow, those who had prayed for him, who had visited him, written to him, encouraged him and, I am sure, believed that they would never see him well again, heard him thank them for what Jesus had been able to do through their faithfulness.

He quoted James 5: 17 and told them of the evening when Alan had laid hands on him and prayed for his healing and, as he said, "not only have I been healed, but my sins have been forgiven."

And then he revealed to them the message the Lord had given him, through his Word, the day the surgeon had told him there was nothing more he could do. As he waited to leave the hospital for the last time, all hope gone, Jacques sat quietly in his room, his Bible open on his lap, and his eyes had fallen upon Psalm 30. And that Sunday morning in church he read in a strong firm voice:

"I praise you, Lord, because you have saved me and kept my enemies from gloating over me. I cried to you for help, O Lord my God, and you healed me; you kept me from the grave. I was on my way to the depths below, but you restored my life ... You have changed my sadness into a joyful dance; you have taken away my sorrow and surrounded me with joy. So I will not be silent; I will sing praise to you, Lord, you are my God, I will give you thanks for ever."

And when, at Jacques' request, we rose and sang "Thine be the Glory", for the second time in two years I saw tears glistening on the cheeks of the congregation of that little English church.

I think that, for many who knew Jacques and loved him, his healing brought a deeper insight into their Christian walk. Many admitted that they had changed, that Jesus had become more real to them, a presence whom they could talk to and appeal to – a living person with whom they could walk in their daily life and not just part of the ritual of the Anglican prayer book.

From that moment onwards, the church was wide open for the breath of the Spirit and a new wind blew through that historic building and lives began to be changed.

In our own family those who didn't believe could find no explanation and merely turned away, shaking their heads. Bee, our sweet-natured, lovely girl, someone the "world" would describe as a "real Christian", had fallen away in her teens and, like Olivier, not returned. But she had done so in her own gentle fashion, without violence, without arguments or rebellion. Almost without our noticing it, she had just slipped through our fingers and, though she never put it into so many words, we knew that she no longer believed.

But she loved her father dearly and when he told her of his healing she looked at him unbelievingly then went over and pulled at his shirt front which for over two years had hidden the wad of cotton wool and bandages. When she saw the healthy skin and the scar, her hands dropped and she gasped, then her enormous brown eyes looked up at him incredulously, almost fearfully, before she turned and, without a word, walked out of the room. She never mentioned it again, but I know that moment went deep. The evidence was there, and there was no "rational" explanation.

Our lives took on a new dimension. We had gone to a meeting shortly before his healing where Jacques had received the baptism of the Spirit and been given a beautiful new language by the Lord: the first time in our lives when he had been "spiritually" behind me. And now that we were both more on fire than ever, our door was opened even wider and I understood that if one is faithful in prayer and willing to be used, it is not necessary to race around trying to do God's work: Jesus sends the people who need to know. At least, that is how it was with us. And as we drew more deeply at his well of wisdom, so Jesus opened the doors he wanted opened and closed those which were not for us.

Not long after Jacques' healing, Bee came to us one evening dragging a tall, blond young man behind her. He was a perfect foil for her petite dark beauty and they reminded me of Anne and Charles as I had first known them. Hervé, a former schoolfriend and namesake of her brother, had been haunting the house and telephone for a couple of years, so it didn't surprise me when she announced that they were engaged. He was due to sit his finals that summer and they wanted to marry shortly afterwards.

As I sat with the boys in the dim, crowded church the following June, I turned as the organ broke into Handel's "Water Music" to see Bee coming down the aisle clinging to Jacques' arm, a beautiful dream floating in a sea of white tulle, radiant with happiness as she went to meet her bridegroom. And I could not help remembering the last time I had consciously listened to the pealing bells of this old seventeenth-century church at the top of the hill. My mind went back two and a half years to the morning when I had awakened to their ringing and felt such peace, knowing that I had totally surrendered all that I held most dear to Jesus. I looked at Jacques as he neared the altar and handed over his precious charge into another man's keeping, marvelling at what had happened in his life, in all our lives. As Hervé and Bee joined their hands in the shimmering golden ray coming through the stained-glass window and falling on their bowed heads, tears of pure joy filled my eyes and threatened to stream down my cheeks.

Yves looked up, embarrassed, and nudged me.

"Don't *cry*," he whispered fiercely.

At almost fifteen, he was becoming very self-conscious.

"You did, last night," I whispered back.

He reddened. The evening before we had all been in a flurry of last-minute preparations, putting the final touches to the house, the garden, the marquee and rearranging the enormous vases of flowers which were everywhere in readiness for the reception when, suddenly, I had found Yves sobbing quietly in a corner of the garden.

"Whatever's the matter?" I asked, bewildered.

He had seemed so happy all day, as indeed we all had been, working busily under Olivier's expert organisation.

"I've lost my sister," he gulped.

I didn't know what to say. He and Bee had always been very close, even as children, but since he had returned to school in France the year before the age gap seemed to have closed. Although he was very fond of his future brother-in-law, he doubtless realised, as I did when I stopped to think, that this was the end of an era in our lives and when she came home again it would be different.

But as if she sensed his distress, Bee appeared and sat down on the grass beside him.

"Yves," she said gently, understanding him better than I did and not at all bewildered by the situation, "I'll always be your sister."

"Yes," he gulped again, "but after tomorrow you won't be a Riols any more."

She smiled and put her arms round him, rubbing her cheek against his.

"I'll always be a Riols," she answered softly, as I crept away leaving them together in the warm glow of the fairy lights which had been hidden in the trees especially for the following evening's festivities.

And now tomorrow, the great day we had all been working towards, had arrived and, in a few minutes, she would indeed no longer be a Riols. But as I looked at her radiant face gazing up at her future husband as they

exchanged their vows, I knew that it didn't matter at all by
what name we are called, to which family we belong, to
which country we owe allegiance. The only important thing
is that we are members of the family of God and can call
ourselves Christians.

Jacques went forward to read the passage he had chosen
for the occasion, 1 Corinthians, chapter 13, and I prayed
that Jesus would pour that love of which it spoke into their
hearts for each other. And that when the excitement of the
day and the passion of the honeymoon was over, they would
settle down and know this beautiful love which is "patient
and kind, not conceited or jealous or proud, ill-mannered,
selfish or irritable; not keeping a record of wrongs, not
happy with evil but happy with the truth. Love which never
gives up, whose faith, hope and patience never fail. Love
which is eternal."

That summer of 1977 was thrilling for us all. So many
things had happened in our lives, and preparations were
being made for further changes. My father came to stay and
everything culminated in a grand finale in September when
for the second time in three months, we were all together as a
family, a family which was joyfully expanding.

Our Hervé had married his Cécile two years earlier and
now, his student days over, was about to leave with his wife
and baby daughter, Clémence, our first grandchild, to take
up an appointment in Dakar. Olivier had returned from
troubled Beirut and was installed in happy bachelordom in a
flat in Paris, and Hervé and Bee were leaving that week for
Morocco where they were to live for two years.

My brother and his family came over from Normandy to
join us and that golden September weekend the house and
garden rang with our happiness as endless photos were taken
and the young people teased and laughed together.

But, as so often happens when we reach a peak in our
secular as well as our spiritual life, we come rushing quickly
down the other side of the mountain very soon afterwards.
Perhaps God does this so that we may not become self-
satisfied or boast, or maybe it is the devil, but whatever it is
the following Saturday saw us down to earth again with a
bump.

Even in my pre-Christian days I had never really wanted

deep down to be a liberated wife and although, before I met Jesus, I had grumbled often enough about having no time to myself or never "being myself", whatever that may mean, I think I would have been horrified if I had had to take the consequences and the responsibilities attached to being "free". Figures have always eluded me and it was Jacques who coped with the family finances and supplied all my needs – not always my wants, but certainly my needs, and I was more than happy to leave it that way. But when he was taken ill, gearing the family budget fell to me and I didn't make a very good job of it. Maybe I should have had a hand in it before. With hindsight one can change so many things, but the fact was that I had never had to cope and when I was forced into that position it was like a heavy chain hanging round my neck.

Hervé was the first to help me out when he arrived from Montpellier two days after Jacques' operation. He sorted through all kinds of papers which were incomprehensible to me and set me on the right road but, unfortunately, after he left I let myself get into a muddle. Olivier came back from Beirut that summer for a quick visit to see what he could do to help and spent a great deal of time with paper clips and bank statements putting everything in order, ringing up here, there and everywhere and setting me on my feet again. But although I meant to try to keep some kind of order, hell is paved with good intentions and I added several financial paving stones during those fateful two years.

When Jacques was healed, I think our finances must have been in a pretty poor state for, although the social security paid everything, there had been an awful lot of extras I had had to provide, like private rooms when my husband was so desperately ill and all the incidental expenses incurred when the head of the house is stricken. Money had never meant a great deal to us and when a life is at stake it becomes even less important.

And then, just at the time when Jacques was able, physically, to take over the reins and try to sort out our crumbling finances, Bee announced her engagement and forthcoming marriage and the coffers had to be delved into again. We never for one moment regretted it: her wedding was a perfect souvenir of us as a family all working together towards this wonderful send-off for our precious daughter. But it had not helped our bank balance.

So when, on the Saturday morning after the party, the bank manager telephoned and Jacques casually mentioned that he was popping in to see him, although I knew our finances were not as healthy as they should be, we had been "in the red" before and I wasn't unduly worried.

When my husband walked back into the house, I was standing in the hall thumbing through the morning's post, and looked up in surprise. I hadn't expected him back so soon. He'd promised to take the dogs for a walk in the forest, yet here they were, yapping at his heels as he closed the front door.

"I've something I want to discuss with you," he said, steering me towards the drawing-room.

And he told me about his interview with the bank manager.

We were thirteen thousand francs overdrawn and unless the money was in the bank by that afternoon, the manager was threatening to return all our cheques marked "RD".

I'm afraid I was more upset than Jacques was, which didn't help. In actual fact, Jacques didn't appear to be upset at all. To him money has always been something God gave us to be used, not left lying in a bank, but between that and finding ourselves head over heels in debt...

"What are you going to do?" I asked numbly.

"What I told the bank manager I'd do," he replied evenly. "Pray about it."

I looked at him in astonishment.

"You didn't tell him that?" I asked unbelievingly.

"Of course I did," Jacques continued. "What else did you expect me to say? He wanted some sort of guarantee that the money would be there and I had none to give him, so when he asked me what I intended to do, I told him. Unless," he added with a twinkle in his eye, "you have some other solution?"

I hadn't.

"What did he say?" I ventured, not daring to imagine.

"Oh, he thought I was quite mad," Jacques continued airily, "said I obviously didn't realise the seriousness of the situation and that being flippant wouldn't help at all."

I nodded without replying; it was the sort of answer I

expected he would give.

"I told him," Jacques went on more gravely, "that it was because I *did* realise its seriousness that I was going home to pray about it."

It was Christopher's last weekend before returning to school for the autumn term. Yves was preparing to re-attack his studies on the following Monday, all their friends were around and the house was humming with their comings and goings as Jacques and I knelt together on the drawing-room floor.

"Oh Lord," he said quietly, "I've got us into this awful mess financially and, at this moment, I don't see any way out. But you told us in your Word to bring all our worries to you and, just as we have always done, this morning once again I ask you please to give me the solution. Humanly speaking, there isn't one, but we know that with you all things are possible."

And his hand reached for mine as we knelt in silence.

As we got up from our knees, Jacques threw his arm round my shoulders and drew me close to him.

"It *is* wonderful to be able to pray together, isn't it?" he smiled.

I just nodded. It wasn't the first time he had said that and my heart was very full.

"Anything interesting in the mail?" Jacques said, breaking the silence and stretching out his hand for the letters I had just picked up again.

"Doesn't look like it," I replied, leafing through them. "Just the usual. Oh, here's a letter from a clinic in the Drôme. Do you know anyone down there?"

"No," he replied laconically, "let's have a look."

I handed him the envelope and began slitting open the others. He let out a low whistle.

"Just listen to *this*," he said incredulously, sitting down abruptly on the window-seat and beginning to read out loud.

The letter was from a lawyer announcing that the clinic had changed hands and the shares which Jacques' father had bought when the clinic had been built were now available. Did Jacques, as his father's sole heir, wish to cash or reinvest them? They totalled eighteen and were worth five hundred francs each.

We just stared at each other, and couldn't believe it!

"Well," said my husband slowly, "that's nine thousand francs."

"But we still need four thousand more," I said warily, mentally taking back the problem we had so recently handed over to God. "What are we going to do?"

"Have lunch," replied my practical husband. "I'm beginning to feel hungry, aren't you?"

And he went off, happily whistling, across the garden.

The mere thought of food choked me, but I went into the kitchen and began mechanically taking pots and pans down from the shelf. It was warm and cosy, the air was full of pungent cooking smells and I felt comforted by the familiarity of it all as I bent to pop the pastry into the oven.

"Can you boys set the table," I called over my shoulder at the clatter of feet racing down the stairs, "and find Daddy and tell him lunch won't be long."

At that moment the telephone rang.

"Oh Mum," said Christopher, coming into the kitchen. "I'm awfully sorry, but it's Georges on the telephone."

"What are you sorry about?" I enquired, going to pick up the receiver.

"No, but Mum, wait," Christopher went on. He seemed embarrassed. "I don't think he's very pleased. He rang you last night and asked me to be sure to tell you to ring him back first thing this morning and I completely forgot. Sorry," he ended lamely as I brushed past him and picked up the phone.

"Hallo, Georges," I answered brightly. "Sorry I didn't call you back, but Christopher has only just given me the message."

"Well, it *was* rather urgent," he replied. "Do you remember that ring you gave me a couple of years ago?"

I did remember. It had belonged to a great-aunt of mine whom I had never known and, as it had no particular sentimental value, I had asked Georges, our jeweller friend, to sell it for me. And, in the meantime, I had forgotten all about it.

"I wanted to get hold of you as soon as possible," Georges went on, "because I have a client who's interested. That marquise setting is apparently just what his wife has always wanted and he's been looking for one for some time. I told you it was unusual, didn't I, and wouldn't be as easy to sell as the classic diamond setting. The thing is, he's leaving this evening so I need an answer straight away."

"How much is he offering?" I asked cautiously, my heart jumping into my throat and starting to pound uncontrollably.

"Four thousand francs," Georges replied. "If you're interested, I'd accept it. It's a good price and I may have to wait another couple of years before I get another direct sale."

My voice seemed to come from a long way off.

"I'll take it," I said, not daring to ask when we could hope to have the money.

"Oh good," Georges answered brightly. "I'm glad that's settled. By the way, we're coming out to Etang for the weekend."

He and his wife had a cottage in the village next to ours.

"With a bit of luck, we may get there for a late lunch: I'll pop the cheque into you on the way, we've got to pass the house," he ended. "See you in about an hour."

And he rang off.

As I turned to go back into the kitchen, I heard Jacques' cheerful whistling coming back across the garden, and words from the Book of Proverbs came to my mind:

"Trust in the Lord with all thine heart and lean not to thine own understanding. In all thy ways acknowledge him and he will direct thy path."

"Forgive me, Lord," I murmured. "And thank you."

The manager looked enquiringly at Jacques as he walked cheerily into his office when the bank opened after the lunchtime break.

"There you are," said my irrepressible husband as he laid the equivalent of thirteen thousand francs on the desk in front of him. "A cheque for four thousand and nine thousand in shares ready to be cashed."

For a moment there was silence, then, without raising his eyes from the papers in front of him, the manager said, almost inaudibly:

"How did you do it?"

"Exactly as I told you I would," replied my husband quietly. "I went home and prayed."

It was Saturday afternoon, a busy time at the bank, but the manager picked up his phone and asked not to be disturbed then, leaning across his desk, he said incredulously:

"I want to know more; I can't believe it!"

So, very simply, Jacques shared Jesus with this man who had put his faith in figures – and he listened. When Jacques left, he offered the bank manager the pocket New Testament he always carries around with him, and he not only accepted it but promised to read it.

It "just happened", as it so often does in our Christian walk, that the film *The Cross and the Switchblade* was being shown in our local town hall that week and when Jacques mentioned this to him he wasn't surprised to see not only the bank manager but his wife and children sitting in the audience.

> *Oh, put God to the test and see how kind he is! See for yourself the way his mercies shower down on all who trust in him.*
> *(Psalm 34: 8) (The Living Bible)*

20

LIFE WITHOUT END

Bee and Hervé's two years in Morocco stretched into four and it was during their third year that we received the wonderful news that she was expecting their longed-for child.

They had been home for holidays each summer and were blissfully happy together, but this news confirmed to us that, at last, their union would be complete. We rejoiced with them, especially when she wrote that she wanted to have her baby in France and would be home by mid-June.

She arrived, large and radiant as ever, sailing happily through what looked like the perfect pregnancy – she had not even felt sick! Christopher was now back home at school in France and when, in July, Hervé arrived to join his wife, we left to take Christopher and a friend down to the house in Narbonne where Olivier and, more importantly as far as his brother was concerned, his wind surfer had promised to join us.

Yves didn't want to come, Hervé was working in Paris and Yves preferred to stay at home and "look after" Bee who would otherwise be alone during the day. We didn't insist, knowing what a joy it was for him to have his sister to himself, and left knowing we would be back before the end of August when the baby was due.

Jacques was expected back in his office on Monday, August 18th, and we had decided to drive slowly home, arriving in Marly on the previous Saturday or even the Sunday. But on the Wednesday before, I suddenly felt I wanted to go home and suggested we leave the following morning. We had had a good holiday and nobody really minded, though they couldn't understand my whim any more than I could, so we rang that evening and told Bee we were on our way.

"You're not coming home for me, are you?" she enquired. "I'm perfectly all right, saw the doctor yesterday and he said it won't be before another two weeks."

This was August 13th.

"Oh no," I said; nothing had been farther from my mind. "I'm quite happy to come home and so are Daddy and the boys as it happens, and we'll avoid the weekend traffic if we leave tomorrow. We'll probably stay somewhere overnight, maybe at Tante Lilette's; don't worry if we're not back."

"I won't," she laughed.

And rang off.

We didn't hurry the next morning, knowing we had plenty of time in front of us to attack the nine hundred odd kilometres which separated us from home. So Jacques was more surprised than ever when, as he was consulting the map before setting off, deciding which one of his numerous cousins we'd drop in on for the night, I said, feeling increasingly foolish:

"Would you mind if we went straight to the motorway and did the whole journey in one day?"

He looked at me quizzically.

"You mean just belt home?" he enquired.

I nodded.

"It's a long drive," he demurred. "It'll be killing in this heat."

But something spurred me on.

"I'll take turns driving," I volunteered.

Usually I slept and Jacques did all the driving. He preferred it that way, but seeing I had this strange bee in my bonnet, he merely shrugged.

"All right," he gave in. "If you're prepared to take over, we'd better get started immediately. All right with you, boys?"

"Yes," came a chorus from the back.

I knew they wouldn't mind; tourism had never been one of Christopher's pastimes and once in the car he liked to get to the other end as quickly as possible. So we set off and, as Jacques put it, "belted along the motorway in all that heat". There was a sudden unaccountable urgency in me and I didn't understand why.

We arrived home, exhausted, just after nine, glad to be

back in the cool, and found Yves, Bee and Hervé sitting in the garden in the summer twilight chatting together. We exchanged news and greetings and just when everyone was yawning and considering going off to bed, Bee called me urgently from the bathroom. I rushed upstairs to find her waters had broken.

Now I understood why I had needed to get home.

It must have been midnight when we all stood in the road and waved goodbye as Hervé drove his wife to the hospital. She was as happy as on her wedding day just three years before and I remember waking the next morning with a thrill of excitement, realising that before the day was out Bee would have her baby.

I was unable to settle to anything and, as the day advanced, my excitement and longing to see this new little grandchild grew with every minute. At three o'clock I could stand the waiting no longer and rang through to her room, tentatively suggesting that I should come.

"I'm sure she'd love to see you," Hervé answered. "The midwife has just been in; they're going to give her something to help it along."

Jacques gave me a long, hard look as I put down the phone.

"Now, don't interfere," he said. "This is *their* baby and *their* experience. Let them live it together, their way."

I didn't argue, I just wanted to get there. It seemed to me that even for a first baby it was trailing rather a long time, though what I imagined I could do I didn't know.

"Can I come with you?" Christopher asked when he heard where I was going. He was feeling slightly left out and alone.

Yves, his "responsibility" over, had left that morning for Clermont-Ferrand to stay with Hérve and Cécile, who had returned from Dakar and now had two little daughters, Clémence and Marie. I hesitated.

"Why don't we all go?" Jacques put in quietly. "I've just got one or two things to finish, then I'll be with you."

I fumed with impatience, the minutes were passing and now that I had finally been given permission, I wanted to get there as quickly as possible.

When we arrived at the hospital, Christopher ran ahead down the long corridor, anxious to see his sister, but within seconds he had doubled back.

"How is she?" I asked brightly.

"She's not there," he said blankly. "But Hervé is, and he looks funny."

For a moment my heart took a desperate leap and then started beating frantically as I saw Hervé, wearing a long white gown, walking towards us. He looked drunk.

I broke into a run.

"Hervé," I gasped as I rushed towards him. "What's happened?"

He looked at me, his eyes glazed and unbelieving.

"She's dead," he said hoarsely.

I stood there, stunned.

"What do you mean?" I gasped. "Tell me what's happened."

"It's the baby," he went on blankly, "a little girl. She's dead."

And, as I gathered his long, lean frame into my arms, his head fell on my shoulder and our tears mingled, hot and anguished, there in the middle of that sterile corridor.

Jacques came up behind us and I turned towards him, a blind anger against the hospital rising in my heart. Hervé walked away into the small waiting room and sat, his head in his hands; Christopher, tears streaming down his face, went and sat down beside him. Jacques took my arm and led me to join them.

I sank on to the bench. Inside me was nothing but a cold, black anger and fear, clutching and squeezing at my heart and draining it of all feeling. And I knew that I could do nothing except sit and suffer quietly alongside these two people whom I loved so much. I could not help them, all I could do was suffer with them.

We saw the surgeon, we saw the obstetrician, the midwife, the nurse on duty, but they closed ranks and there was no explanation except that it was a public holiday. August 15th is the deadest day on the Paris calendar when everyone is away, the unit had been short staffed and had not realised that Bee needed a caesarian until it was too late. The baby was a perfect seven-pound little girl, but by the time they had realised the danger her heart had already stopped beating.

All these explanations did nothing to help us, but it kept

us busy whilst we waited for Bee to come round from the anaesthetic, kept us from wondering how we were going to break the dreadful news to her. Finally a nurse came towards Hervé.

"Your wife would like to see you," she said.

He went into her room and we silently waited. When he came out, we looked up at him expectantly.

"She'd like to see you," he said to me, so not knowing what to say we all four trooped into the room.

Seeing Bee lying there, deathly pale with a bottle hanging upside down by her head, was too much for Christopher. With tears once again streaming down his face he crossed to the window and Jacques followed and stood beside him, an arm thrown protectively round his shaking shoulders. And they stood together, looking vacantly out over the roofs of the buildings opposite, watching a large red sun sink slowly below the horizon.

I sat down by the bed, not knowing what to say, praying that God would give me the words she needed to hear, but knowing that no words could fill the void or instantly heal the deep wound of waking up to find her arms empty.

She looked up at me and her eyes were wide and frightened like those of a fawn, hunted and afraid.

"I want to see my baby," she whispered. "Bring me my baby."

Somehow God gave me the grace and strength not to break down. I leant forward and took her hand and tried to explain that this longed-for baby had died. But she just stared at me, unbelievingly, tears streaming down her cheeks.

"She's not dead," she pleaded. "She was kicking so hard, she can't be dead. Let me see my baby."

Hervé gathered her into his arms, murmuring soft endearments. Helpless and dazed, we crept from the room knowing that there was nothing we could do for either of them at that moment except leave them alone together with their grief.

"Oh God," I cried brokenly as we crossed to the car, "why did you have to do this to her?"

Jacques' grip tightened on my arm.

"God didn't do it," he replied quietly. "It was man."

I had to agree with him, but I couldn't help adding:

"Whatever mistakes man made, God could have righted them. He could have breathed into that little body and made her live."

"He could," Jacques replied, "but he didn't and we must just trust."

I knew he was right, but my mind filled with "if onlys".

If only there had been more staff on duty, if only the doctor had been called more quickly. If only they had realised even half an hour earlier that Bee needed a caesarian, that lovely little baby girl would now be lying in a cot beside her mother's bed instead of on a slab in the hospital mortuary.

Satan had really got me where he wanted me, on my back, angry with God, and he was quietly feeding my anguish. That night as I tried to sleep, I heard only Bee crying for her baby and the next morning when we went back to the hospital and saw her lying there, her face swollen with weeping, my heart nearly broke and I learned one of life's hardest lessons. That there comes a time when one can no longer suffer *for* one's children, one can only stand helplessly aside and suffer *with* them.

When she was a little girl, I used to dry her tears and say, "Don't cry, I'll make it better", but now nothing I could say or do would make any difference.

That night I tossed and turned again and the devil had a heyday.

"You were a nurse," he said, "why didn't you go in to see her earlier? If you'd been there, you'd have seen the signs before it was too late. You could have called the midwife or the doctor, anyone. She's so small it was obvious she'd need a caesarian... but *you* were at home. You shouldn't have listened to your husband when he told you not to interfere. What did he know about it? Now look what's happened, she's gone through that caesarian for nothing."

That was Satan's final jibe – and it hit home! He was really sowing a wonderful harvest for himself. Not only had he convinced me that I could have prevented the tragedy, he had almost persuaded me that it was Jacques' fault that I hadn't!

I flung myself out of bed and on to my knees. Seeing my

distress, Jacques came and knelt beside me, slipping his arm through mine and holding tightly to my hand.

"God," I cried, "I can't stand it. Tell me I'm not responsible. Tell me there was nothing I could have done to save that little life. Take this guilt away and give me your peace."

And I burst into helpless sobbing.

Jacques continued to pray quietly by my side. I knew that he had not stopped holding me up to God ever since he realised that to my sorrow I had added this self-imposed guilt.

My tears spent, I climbed wearily back into bed . . . and fell asleep. The next morning when I awoke, the heaviness of heart, the hurt and the sorrow were still there, but over-riding them was a deep peace. And, as before at times of pain and bewilderment in my life, I turned at random to God's Word and his hand guided and comforted me. Proverbs 20 fell open before my eyes.

"Since the Lord is directing our steps, why try to understand everything that happens along the way?"

And as I read it, the last words from Matthew's Gospel flashed into my mind.

"Lo, I am with you always, even unto the end of the world."

Jacques had gone back to his office so I went to the hospital alone early that morning and as I entered her room Bee smiled at me and, for the first time in three days, I smiled too. As I helped her to wash and put on a clean nightie, little things I had not done for her since she was a child, I suddenly felt very close to her. She seemed more relaxed and began to talk about the baby, something she had been unable to do till then, and I felt that there had been a release in her too. Her pain and grief were deep and raw, but she had no bitterness or anger.

"These things happen, and it has happened to us," she said quietly and, as she looked up at her husband who had just come into the room, she held out her hand to him and there seemed to be a new depth of love and understanding between them.

I was humbled by the unknown depths in our children and the way they so often surprise us. Here she was, living through the worst experience any young mother can be called upon to face and doing so calmly and with a courage I had never dreamed she possessed.

We had prayed very especially for them both when we learned that Bee was expecting a baby; could this prayer bank have opened its doors and poured out the stored blessings on her, helping her to face this tragedy in her young life with such composure? And I marvelled once again at the power of prayer.

Living through this experience brought us even closer together as a family, and her four brothers showed her an unaccustomed tenderness. We had taken it for granted that they loved her, but they had not always openly showed it. But now, each in his own way, through bunches of flowers, embarrassed little notes or visits to the hospital, made her aware of his love and I think even Jacques and I entered into a new depth in our relationship. On the Sunday after the baby died, we sat in the garden all afternoon, talking, not about anything in particular, just chatting, a thing we hadn't found time to do recently. And we both said afterwards that we had felt the need to be together and communicate in order to help us cope with our sorrow.

On the evening before Hervé and Bee returned to Morocco for their last year, we had a joyous family dinner party. Hervé and Cécile came up from Clermont-Ferrand and once again, for the first time in three years, we were all together. And, although no one put it into words, we all knew that the death of Bee's baby had shaken us up as a family and made us realise how precious we all were to one another. I knew their homecoming wasn't going to be easy; the empty cot, the waiting pram, the embarrassed avoidance of the subject by their friends and neighbours, yet I felt at peace about them because I could see that they were looking forwards and not backwards. My eyes were on Jesus who "maketh all things new". And, above all, that he can make something beautiful out of man's mistakes if we will only let him.

It was after this tragedy that the Lord showed us the next step he wanted us to take in our service for him, when he gave Jacques the vision of a fellowship group in our home. This was to be different from the Monday evening Bible Studies which had flourished before Jacques' illness. Now we wanted to attract the unbeliever, the seeker, the doubter, who would never come to a meeting that was specifically for Bible Study. So the accent was to be on praise and sharing, singing and worship, with prayer and a Bible message at the end. We argued for weeks as to the most appropriate evening and finally decided that it is impossible to find a time which suits everybody and we must just make a decision and start. Which we did. We were obedient, did as Jesus prompted us to do and he brought us the people, and now our Friday evenings are flourishing. Through this group we have made friends with people we would never have come into contact with otherwise, and as one person brought another the whole thing snowballed. We have discovered what a wonderful ministry there is in reaching out in love to others, opening our doors and saying "come in and share what we have". And, as Jesus promised, that love we gave has been returned a thousandfold, pressed down and flowing over.

I wonder whether, without my husband's illness, we would have come so far along our Christian walk? I think Jacques would, but I am not so sure that I would have done. I began to understand the meaning of the parable that with faith as big as a grain of mustard seed one can remove mountains and I discovered that it often means the mountains in our lives. Those mountains we sometimes create for ourselves, often out of molehills, and that faith, the tiniest little speck of faith, can remove these insuperable obstacles and show us the way ahead.

I also began to understand that suffering in itself is a part of life. Everyone suffers to some degree or other and it is not necessarily a negative emotion: it all depends on what one does with it. If one can hand it over to Jesus, as Jacques did, then it can transform not only one's own life but also the lives around. Many people were watching Jacques and his reactions to his illness and many were bewildered, even humbled, by his patient acceptance and came to know the Lord because of it. His was not a wasted experience.

I learned, too, that there is a freedom in obedience, a freedom I could never find anywhere else. Sometimes when the Lord would prompt me to do something for him, go somewhere or approach someone, I would react negatively, afraid of ridicule. But I never had peace until I capitulated and did his bidding. In obeying I discovered I was carrying out the orders he had given me, but that the final responsibility was not mine. It was God's.

If Jesus told me to talk to someone about him I could only sow the seed, the Holy Spirit was responsible for it growing in that person's heart. Jesus was the great commander-in-chief, I was merely a simple soldier carrying out orders, and it gave me a wonderful feeling of security... and freedom.

Through it all I learned to appreciate more and more the verse in Romans 8, verse 28, which has become a favourite of mine and one I have clung to in many difficult situations in our life. "I know that all things work for good..." We obey and he carries the promise through.

I claim this promise particularly for the children. Jesus has taught me to bring them up with a long-term vision, seeing them as he sees them in infinity, the new creation. For the whole of our lives, parents have to be a beacon, a light the children can follow, a haven they can come to in dark moments. We have to continue to be their rock and their lighthouse, even though they may never admit it, and we may never see the fruits of the seeds of faith we have tried to sow in this life.

Jesus wants each one of our children to follow him, and if we have done our task properly I feel confident that sooner or later, though we may not perhaps have the joy of seeing it here on earth, he will draw them to him, and they will not be able to resist his call of love. And I know that I have to be patient and trust, for God is not a liar. What he has promised, he carries out.

I will seek my lost ones, those who strayed away, and bring them safely home again.
(Ezekiel 34: 16) (The Living Bible)

21

OUT OF THE TUNNEL

Another Friday evening prayer and praise meeting was over.

I was tidying the drawing-room, and Jacques was listening to the late-night news. The television gave out depressing reports of strikes, wars and deaths, a living tableau of man's inhumanity to man, as I went round rearranging chairs, puffing cushions and slipping the nest of tables back into place.

This was the autumn of 1982. The Beirut fighting, uprisings in Africa, massacres in Iran and Chile and the never-ending Northern Ireland conflict were daily news items. And we had almost ceased to be horrified by them.

I sat down abruptly beside my husband, the joy of the evening draining away and a feeling of desolation taking over as the announcer's voice droned on.

"What a mess," I murmured. "What a hopeless mess we're all in."

Jacques slipped his hand over mine. Even the weather forecast for the weekend was dismal. High winds and storms predicted.

"You're easily discouraged, aren't you?" Jacques said, getting up to switch off the television.

"But the whole world's in turmoil," I protested, the television pictures imprinted vividly on my mind.

"Think back a moment," my husband went on. "How many were in this room not half an hour ago?"

"Eighteen."

"Doesn't that give you hope for the world?" Jacques challenged. "Eighteen of us, from almost as many countries, all worshipping God together. We weren't fighting."

His words cheered me.

It had been a particularly beautiful evening, and one

which I hope had made our Lord's heart rejoice. We'd had a young couple from Martinique, a Ghanaean political refugee, an Australian, a Canadian and two French friends. A shy Indian student had shared his guitar music with a young Oxford graduate as, together, they accompanied our choruses of praise. An American girl had told us very simply and movingly, how she had met Jesus, and a Jewish boy, a convert to Christianity, had sung haunting Hebrew songs, strumming poignant minor chords on his guitar. Before we parted, we had gathered round an octogenarian Englishman who had lost his sight three years before and prayed for it to be restored to him holding hands around the room, had sung "We are one in the bond of love."

"That's where the remedy lies," Jacques said. "We can't change the world by ourselves, but if we each reach out in love where we are, it wouldn't take long for all nations to be at peace."

We sat looking into the dying fire in a comfortable silence.

"Life's a bit like a tunnel," Jacques mused after a while. "From the day we're born we're in it and whilst we're travelling through, it sometimes doesn't seem to make much sense. But we just have to keep our eyes on the light shining at the end, beckoning us forward. And, when we do, life has a meaning because we know that one day we'll burst out of the tunnel into that light and the sunshine of eternity. Then we'll be able to see our short span of time through God's eyes."

He picked up a piece of tapestry I'd been intermittently working on for about ten years.

"It's like this," he went on, warming to his theme. "Down here on earth we're walking about on the wrong side, all mixed up with the knots and joins and imperfections. But God is on the right side of the work, where the pattern is, and he sees the finished picture. We only see the mess – which is where faith comes in. We *know* that God is in control."

He bent down and replaced the tapestry in the basket.

"Having that assurance," he finished quietly, "gives me hope for the future and makes it all worth-while. That's what being a Christian's all about, isn't it?"

I was nodding my head as he spoke. For many years I *hadn't* known what it was all about, but I was eternally thankful that now I did.

Jacques began turning off the lights, and I went over to the window and pulled back the curtain.

The night was very dark, like an endless tunnel, the sky an enveloping deep blue velvet cloak. A solitary star shone through the blackness, shimmering, twinkling as if beckoning me onwards. Words once heard and long since forgotten came back into my mind.

> Look backward with gratitude,
> Look forward with hope,
> Look upwards with confidence.

And I knew the last line held the key.

And this world is fading away, and these evil, forbidden things will go with it, but whoever keeps doing the will of God will live forever.
(I John 2, v. 17.) (Living Bible.)

AS A PARTING WORD

But those who trust in the Lord for help
will find their strength renewed.
They will rise on wings like eagles;
they will run and not get weary;
they will walk and not grow weak.

(Isaiah 40: 31) (Good News Bible)